100 GREATEST ANCIENT COINS

Harlan J. Berk

Foreword by David MacDonald

www.whitmanbooks.com

Whitman Publishing, LLC
Atlanta, GA

100 GREATEST ANCIENT COINS

www.whitman**books**.com

© 2008 Whitman Publishing, LLC
3101 Clairmont Road · Suite C · Atlanta GA 30329

Correspondence concerning this book may be directed to the publisher,
Attn: 100 Greatest Ancient coins, at the address above.

ISBN: 0794822622
Printed in China

To my wife Pam and our children and grandchildren, both biologically and through marriage: Aaron, Jennifer, Shanna, Rainer, Jake, Janice, Darin, Sammy, Malia, Jakob, Ian, Alaina, Leo, Halle, and those to come. Their names will be known as long as a copy of this book exists.

Disclaimer: Expert opinion should be sought in any significant numismatic purchase. This book is presented as a guide only. No warranty or representation of any kind is made concerning the accuracy or completeness of the information presented, or its usefulness in numismatic purchases or sales. The opinions of others may vary. The author is a professional numismatist and regularly buys, sells, and sometimes holds certain of the items discussed in this book.

Caveat: The price estimates given here are subject to variation and differences of opinion. Especially rare coins trade infrequently, and an estimate or past auction price may have little relevance to future transactions. Before making decisions to buy or sell, consult the latest information. Grading of ancient coins is subject to wide interpretation, and opinions can differ. Past performance of the ancient-coin market or any coin or type within that market is not necessarily an indication of future performance. Such factors as changing demand, popularity, grading interpretations, strength of the overall market, and economic conditions will continue to be influences. The market for a given coin can fall or it can rise.

Advertisements within this book: Whitman Publishing, LLC, does not endorse, warrant, or guarantee any of the products or services of its advertisers. All warranties and guarantees are the sole responsibility of the advertiser.

For a complete catalog of numismatic reference books, supplies, and storage products,
visit Whitman Publishing online at www.whitman**books**.com

CONTENTS

FOREWORD

Mythology meets peerless artistry in the gold stater of Lampsacus, from circa 394 to 350 B.C. This remarkable coin portrays the unlucky Actaeon, who was turned into a stag and killed by his own hounds after having spied the goddess Artemis bathing. (Actual size approx. 17 mm)

BY DAVID MACDONALD

The coins of the Greeks and Romans were more than a mere means of financial exchange. They were miniature sculptures through which these ancient peoples represented their deities and ideals, exhibited the artistic sophistication of their communities, and displayed their communal pride.

Since they were first made, ancient coins have been admired and collected. Greek and Roman potters sometimes decorated their vessels with the impressions of coins. Augustus Caesar himself, the first emperor of Rome and ruler at the time of Jesus' birth, gave old coins to friends as New Year's gifts. During the Middle Ages, when much knowledge of the Greco-Roman world was lost, ancient coins still fascinated, sometimes inspired contemporary issues, and even became the subjects of strange myths. During the Renaissance, people consciously turned to the world of Greece and Rome for inspiration, and the appreciation of ancient coins became widespread. Collectors included the greatest rulers and artists of the age. In his autobiography, for example, Benvenuto Cellini, the great goldsmith and sculptor, describes with admiration ancient coins that he was able to acquire. The Enlightenment of the late 17th and 18th centuries also revered the classical world, and outstanding minds of the era collected and studied ancient coins. The growing emphasis on historical methodology in the 19th century led to increasingly scholarly studies, and that tradition continues today. Many of those studies as well as fine auction catalogs are authored by dealers and collectors, true connoisseurs.

Connoisseurship requires both natural gifts and years of study and experience, and Harlan Berk is a true numismatic connoisseur. I have counted him as a good friend for over a quarter of a century and learned much from him. He maintains a large numismatic library, which he makes available to collectors and scholars who visit his offices in Chicago. He has handled virtually every variety of ancient coin from the most common to the unique, including many famous specimens with long and distinguished provenances. His eye for style is unsurpassed, as many of the most discerning collectors for whom he has acquired coins can readily attest. Harlan truly loves ancient coins, their beauty, their historical associations, and, in a word, their mystique.

In short, Harlan is eminently qualified to write this book, but in choosing the hundred coins to write about, he has not relied solely on his own judgment. Rather, Harlan consulted a distinguished group of dealers and collectors to compile the selection. There was a remarkable degree of consensus among the group, and we have before us a distinguished collection of individual masterpieces that also forms a comprehensive whole. These hundred specimens not only exemplify the finest ancient coinage but also constitute an overview of ancient art from the Greek Archaic period, in the seventh century B.C., until the end of the Eastern Roman (or Byzantine) Empire in the mid-15th century A.D.

The average collector, such as I, can afford only a few of the coins included in this book, and even the most wealthy could not acquire many of the rarest, but Harlan Berk together with Whitman Publishing has given us all the next best thing: the opportunity to see and appreciate excellent illustrations of splendid specimens of the best ancient coins.

100 *Greatest Ancient Coins* is the fifth entry in Whitman Publishing's 100 Greatest™ library. It follows books that showcase coins, currency notes, medals and tokens, and stamps of the United States—in fact, it is the first title of the 100 Greatest family to focus on non–U.S. collectibles. This reflects Whitman's solid background in world-coin and ancient-coin numismatics. *100 Greatest Ancient Coins* joins such works as *Coins of the Bible* (Friedberg), the *Handbook of Ancient Greek and Roman Coins* (Klawans), and the award-winning *Money of the Bible* (Bressett). It also heralds newer books in the field, such as *Collecting Ancient Greek Coins* (Rynearson) for beginning and intermediate collectors, and the *Guide Book of Overstruck Greek Coins: Studies in Greek Chronology and Monetary Theory* (MacDonald) for more advanced students.

DETERMINING THE 100 GREATEST

The coins that occupy the 100 Greatest roster were voted into place by a survey of distinguished museum curators, historians, coin dealers, researchers, and collectors. The coins are not necessarily the most valuable or the most rare, but those that embody a winning combination of rarity, value, historical significance, beauty, popularity, and other characteristics. Our voters were not constrained, nor were they pre-instructed, in how to gauge each coin's "greatness." That measurement was left up to them, in order to gather rankings as unique and varied as the individual voters.

Often, of course, the factors in an ancient coin's greatness are interrelated. For example, a coin recognized for its connection to a world-famous event will be a perennial favorite among collectors. Such popularity leads to increasing interest as every newcomer to the hobby looks for an example for his collection. Following the law of supply and demand (they're certainly not making any more of these coins!), increased interest will lead to higher market prices. Thus history, popularity, and value intertwine. The coin ranked No. 1, the "Ides of March" denarius, offers an extreme example—with yet another factor added to the equation: rarity. Every collector knows the story of Brutus's assassination of Julius Caesar, but fewer than 100 will be able to own one of the ancient coins struck to commemorate that dramatic act. There are about 80 in existence, and they regularly sell for $100,000 or more.

In a different situation, a coin might have tremendous popularity but exist in such quantities that most collectors, on most budgets, can acquire a specimen. One example is the Aegina silver stater, famous for its depiction of a sea turtle. This is a "beginner" coin for many ancient-coin collections—popular and historical, but common enough and relatively inexpensive at $200 or so in Fine condition. It takes its place high among the 100 Greatest as No. 16.

Of those coins voted the 100 Greatest, ranking among the top three positions was the most hotly contested, with their mathematically calculated "scores" varying by only a few points. The Brutus Eid Mar denarius (No. 1) scored 1,792; the classic Athens decadrachm scored 1,783; and the beautiful Euainetos decadrachm scored 1,767. At the midpoint, No. 50 (the "Tribute Penny" of Tiberius) scored 967; and at the bottom of the ranking, No. 100 (a coin of the short-reigned Byzantine emperor Michael V) scored 342.

LAYOUT AND PRESENTATION

100 Greatest Ancient Coins differs in its format from other books in Whitman's 100 Greatest collection. Following discussion with the author, we have made the editorial decision to present each coin not in its *rank* order, but in its chronological order. (For the curious, a separate table of contents on page iv lists the coins according to rank.) Chronological arrangement allows the reader to follow the history not only of Western Civilization, but of coinage itself—seeing the rise and fall of popular engraving styles, changes in metallic composition, and other developments across the span of time. An arrangement by rank would have started with No. 1 in 42 B.C. Rome, jumping backward more than 400 years to No. 2 in 465 B.C. Athens, and then forward several decades to Syracuse, and from there back to 460 B.C.—a confusing and illogical route.

A two-page spread is devoted to each of coins No. 1 through No. 10, and Nos. 11 through 100 enjoy a full page. In the banner at the top of each page is the coin's rank; a descriptive title; the city, state, or region from which it hails; and its date of striking (or an approximation). Beneath is an enlarged illustration of the coin; a notation of its actual size in millimeters; a summary of market trends and values; and, ghosted in the background, the numeral(s) of its rank. This is followed by an essay that sets the coin in its historical foundation and describes the virtues of its numismatic greatness. At the bottom of the page, a timeline charts the coin's position in time, with the birth of Christ noted for context.

The book is rounded out by a gallery of relative sizes, showing each coin in its actual diameter; a glossary; a bibliography for further reading; a biography of author Harlan J. Berk; and credits and acknowledgments.

Each coin herein, no matter where it stands among the 100, deservedly ranks as one of the greatest relics of antiquity. Individually each stands out as a unique piece of history, artistry, and human effort. Collectively, they tell the story of civilization from the glory days of the ancient Greeks to the waxing and waning of imperial Rome, and into the sunset of the Byzantine empire, before Europe sank into the Dark Ages.

To own an ancient coin is to hold history in your hand. The hope of Whitman Publishing is that this book—with its dramatic illustrations and engaging narrative—will broaden your existing interest in ancient coins, or perhaps even inspire you to join the hobby as a collector. You will find the pursuit to be very rewarding.

In general, people think of the Greeks and the Romans as the beginning of Western culture, but in reality they are more analogous to the late summer and autumn of the beginning. Western culture began when man first started living in organized communities and creating art—not art in the sense of paintings and sculpture, but the decoration of tools, the creation of small stone or bone pendants, and ritualistic burial. We know now that Neanderthal man did all of these things, and certainly the Cro-Magnon did.

THE BEGINNINGS OF ART AND WRITTEN LANGUAGE

In about 30,000 B.C., the Cro-Magnon created their famous cave paintings in what is now France and Spain. These display a sophisticated understanding of the natural world and what must have been the organized system of beliefs known to us as religion. In the Late Paleolithic and Early Neolithic eras, people began to live a more agrarian lifestyle. With this lifestyle came specialization and increased trade. Since man was no longer forced to rely on hunting and gathering for food, he had time to create art. A variety of different cultures developed, such as the Larissa in Thessaly and Macedonia, the Vinca in Yugoslavia, the Kilia (known as "stargazers") in Turkey, the Kephala in Attica, and the Tel Halaf in Syria.

About 3500 B.C., the Sumerians developed written language, cuneiform, in Mesopotamia; at roughly the same time, the Egyptians created hieroglyphics. These cultures arose in rich river-valley environments, which provided a great deal of food as well as natural transportation, a combination that resulted in great trading centers. These trading centers developed complex cultures and forms of government to control and regulate what had been produced. Over the course of several millennia, these great centers established satellite communities, which evolved slightly differently, leading to the growth of many diverse cultures throughout the Middle East and Europe.

THE BIRTH OF COINAGE

During this time Europe lagged behind the emerging centers of the Near East and had no need for coinage. In the Near East, the Sumerians and Egyptians had developed states so centralized that they too had no need for coinage, and what little private commerce that did take place was settled by barter. Even as time passed and silver came to be widely used in economic exchanges, barter continued to be important. When silver was employed, it usually took the form of irregular pieces, ingots, and jewelry, all of which had to be weighed for each transaction.

From the earliest days of artistic expression, the human form has been a universally popular subject—in early sculptures, like these, and eventually on coins. Shown here are works from the cultures of Neolithic Greece (such as Larissa), Vinca, and Kilia.

The coins of Greece and Lydia started as lumps of electrum and developed from there. Croesus issued the first gold and silver coins, like the staters shown here. (Actual sizes approx. 10, 17, and 20 mm)

About 650 B.C., Greeks living on what is now the west coast of Turkey and the Lydians, a related people who lived inland from the Greek coastal settlements, began to develop coinage. Their civilizations were not centrally organized and had no dominant powers akin to those of the ancient Near Eastern empires, a fact that provided more opportunities for individual economic initiative. The old systems of barter and weighing silver were too cumbersome for these fast-moving entrepreneurs, and so coinage was born.

The first Greek and Lydian coins were mere lumps of electrum, an alloy of gold and silver that occurred naturally in deposits in western Anatolia. The lumps, however, were of regular weight to facilitate commerce, and

The legendary Alexander the Great, portrayed here at the Battle of Issus, issued the silver tetradrachm that ranks as No. 20 in the 100 Greatest—and that may bear Alexander's own likeness. (Actual size approx. 27 mm)

soon they began to develop minimal designs. Simple striations appeared on the obverse, and the mark of the punch used to drive the metal into the die showed on the reverse. Over time, obverse types became more elaborate, depicting animal and human forms. Governments, such as the Lydian monarchy and individual Greek city-states, monopolized the issue of coins. The first gold and silver coins were issued by King Croesus, who reigned from 560 to 546 B.C. (see No. 9 in the 100 Greatest, on pages 12–13). Each gold coin had a corresponding silver coin of the same weight, with a value ratio of 13 to 1. Croesus's coinage thus became the first bimetallic, interrelated coinage and monetary system. With an obverse design of a facing lion (representing strength) and bull (for virility), the coins were still archaic in style, with only a double square punch on the reverse. Nevertheless, the coin types were so carefully developed that prototype or trial pieces, issued before a standard was decided upon, still exist today. After the types were successfully developed, they were strictly adhered to.

Coins were a remarkable success, spreading west and east. In the west, Greek city-states on the Greek mainland, in southern Italy and Sicily, and even in southern France issued coins. In the east, coinage spread more slowly and unevenly. The Persian kingdom, which came to dominate all of the Near East from the west coast of Turkey east to Afghanistan and south through Mesopotamia and Egypt, did issue coins, but mainly for the use of Greeks in their kingdom and groups that did business with them.

Early Greek coins are excellent examples of vigorous Archaic style and are universally acknowledged to be among the most important monuments of early Greek art. See, for example, the early coins of Ephesus, Poseidonia, and Cyzicus (Nos. 61, 26, and 75, respectively; see pages 10, 11, and 14). With the passage of time, the obverse designs of coins grew increasingly elaborate and artistic, and in most Greek city-states the old punch-mark reverse

gave way to new reverse types as elaborate as the obverse. Some of the Greek coins of the late Archaic and classical periods, roughly 525 to 415 B.C., were designed and executed by elite artists at the forefront of stylistic developments, such as Kimon and Euainetos, and certainly rank among the greatest coins ever issued in terms of artistic merit and significance in art history. See, for instance, the brilliant coins struck in this period at Syracuse and other cities in Sicily, as well as southern Italy (referred to as "Magna Graecia"). Among the Syracusan splendors are our No. 5, the magnificent Demareteion decadrachm (pages 20–21); No. 17, the unique Alpheius tetradrachm (page 16); and No. 19, the Arethusa 100-litra coin (page 45).

The classical style continued to develop through the period from 400 to 350 B.C., becoming increasingly confident and elaborately decorative. Notable in this period are the coins of Clazomenae, such as our No. 47 (page 47), and Rhodes, whose tetradrachm is our No. 27 (page 48).

By 350 B.C. the great age of Greek city-states was passing. New kingdoms, so large that no city could compete with them, began to emerge. First, Philip II made Macedonia dominant in Greece, and then his son, Alexander the Great, conquered the Persian Empire. Alexander died young, however, and his generals fought for the rest of their lives to establish a single successor. This proved impossible, and instead three great kingdoms evolved, ruled by the descendants of these generals. These kingdoms acted as the region's chief political forces for the next three centuries. The Ptolemy dynasty controlled Egypt; Lysimachus and then the Antigonid family held Macedonia; and the Seleucid family dominated Syria, Mesopotamia, and lands to the east. In addition, more than half a dozen other kingdoms controlled smaller areas of the eastern Mediterranean, and still more kingdoms arose farther to the east as the major powers began to weaken. The coins of the

The portraiture of early Roman imperial coinage is notable for realism rather than flattery, as can be seen in the likenesses of (left to right) Nero, Vespasian, and Galba. Marcus Aurelius visibly ages on the coins of his reign, two of which are shown here. (Actual sizes approx. 18 to 21 mm)

Rome's first emperor, who took the name Augustus, is one of many famous historical figures to appear on the coinage of the Imperatorial period, such as this silver denarius. (Actual size approx. 20 mm)

Hellenistic kingdoms frequently portray their rulers, and sometimes these depictions rise to the height of great art. The coins of Pharnaces (No. 79, page 69) and Orophernes (No. 82, page 72) are prime examples.

Meanwhile, in the west, the Roman Republic was growing into a major power. From about 260 B.C. until the death of Julius Caesar in 44 B.C., more than 100 moneyers were responsible for more than 900 different coins, as the Roman Republic grew to dominate the entire Mediterranean world. Gold coins included those issued during the Romans' greatest crisis, the conflicts with Carthage (see Nos. 25 and 68, pages 65 and 66); the portrait gold stater of Flamininus, the Roman conqueror of Macedonia (No. 63, page 68); and the gold coinage of Sulla, the generalissimo who became dictator of Rome in the first century B.C. (No. 72, page 73).

Eventually, Rome's republican government became corrupt and failed, to be replaced by a government dominated by one supreme ruler—the emperor. This transition, known as the Imperatorial period, is documented by coins portraying the great names of the age: Julius Caesar, Mark Antony, Cleopatra, Pompey the Great, Brutus, Sextus Pompey, and Octavian, who under the altered name of Augustus ("the one held in awe") became Rome's first emperor.

Portraiture developed throughout this period, and Roman imperial coinage of the first two centuries A.D. is notable for its realistic portraits of emperors and other members of the imperial families. Augustus's portraits uniformly depict him as a young man when he was known as Octavian and as a man in his early 30s throughout his entire long reign, from 27 B.C. until 14 A.D., without any change. In contrast, the portraits of Nero, who reigned from 54 to 68 A.D., develop throughout his life. There is no flattery in these Roman portraits. Galba is a grizzled old man,

Vespasian a tough general, and Marcus Aurelius transitions from an apple-cheeked boy with curly hair to a young man with a slight beard, and finally to an older individual with a drawn face and a long beard. The reverses of all these coins are equally interesting, depicting many different and diverse types. Some display deities and personifications of Roman virtues, others historical buildings or scenes from contemporary history. Unlike the Greeks, most Romans were literate, and coins were a way for the emperors to disseminate information to the citizens. Certain coins, for instance, depict the Roman triumph over the Judean dream of independence, and Trajan's bridge over the Danube; one aureus by Hadrian is dated year 874 from the founding of Rome (121 A.D. of our dating system).

During the reign of Gallienus, from 259 to 268 A.D., silver was removed from coinage, although the silver denominations remained—not unlike the case of today's coinage. The reform of Diocletian in 294 A.D. introduced the pure-silver argenteus, but real portraiture was abandoned for political reasons. Portraiture briefly reemerged under Constantine the Great, especially his Constantinople dedication medallions of 330 A.D. (No. 64, page 111).

After Constantine's reign ended in 337 A.D., coins became increasingly Christianized and the portraits less recognizable as individuals. Those of Magnentius, his brother Decentius, and later Julian II ("the Philosopher"), who wanted to return to the old pagan ways, are rare exceptions. In the portraiture of later coins, the old Roman realism was replaced with a new sense of abstraction that sought to depict the underlying essence without what was thought to be confusing and obscuring detail. To the modern eye, accustomed to photographic realism, this attempt to depict the essential character of the subject can appear dull or even crude, but it is really just a different way of seeing and understanding the world. This new abstraction evolved and developed over the course of time, but remains basic to the art of the "Byzantine" empire (the misnomer used to describe the eastern half of the

Roman coinage had become debased and nearly worthless by the time of Diocletian, who attempted to restore its value with coins like the pure-silver argenteus. (Actual size approx. 20 mm)

Roman Empire that survived after the fall of the western half in the fifth century A.D.). The term *Byzantine* was invented by a papal politician 150 years after the fall of Constantinople. He argued that if Constantinople had been founded on the site of the Greek city of Byzantium by pagan Greeks, then the people of Constantinople must also be Greeks and therefore pagans. The idea was that the seat of Christianity could only be, and could only ever have been, Rome. In fact, the people of the Eastern Empire always referred to themselves as Romans, and the inscriptions on their coinage read, "King of the Romans Under God and Christ."

Since the art of the Byzantine or Eastern Roman Empire was clearly descended from the late Roman style, Byzantine coinage is customarily included in the category of ancient coinage. Contemporary medieval European coinage, which is distinct in style and character, is not.

The Eastern Roman Empire survived for a thousand years after the fall of the west, producing such notable coins as the first and second numismatic portrayals of Christ (Nos. 77 and 93, pages 114 and 115), the magnificent large bronzes of Constantine IV, and the sad, crude silver coins issued by Constantine XI just days—perhaps just hours—before the end of the "Byzantine" Empire with the fall of Constantinople in 1453 (No. 94, page 118).

The distinct differences between Byzantine and medieval European coinage design are evident when one compares this bronze follis of Constantine IV (top) to a silver denar of medieval Hungary. (Actual sizes approx. 35 mm [top] and 14 mm)

The Second Punic War brought heavy losses, both human and monetary. Debased coins with low precious-metal content, such as this tridrachm of Hannibal, testified to the high cost of warfare. (Shown actual size)

COLLECTING ANCIENT COINS

Ancient coins bring the collector, literally, into firsthand contact with the entire ancient Western world. These precious metal objects are messages from the past.

In the case of the Greeks, they let us see what the cities wanted to be known for, who their deities were, and what their accomplishments were—as well as their failures (e.g., the debased tridrachms issued by Hannibal after the Second Punic War).

In the Hellenistic Era, from Philip II to Cleopatra VII, we see the kings and queens of that 300-year period as they wanted to be viewed by their subjects and rivals.

During the Roman Republic, coins first portrayed the chief deity, Roma; later the republic's mythology and deities; and later still the accomplishments of the moneyer's ancestors. In the Imperatorial and Imperial periods, coinage portrayed, sometimes with brutal accuracy, the emperors and their families and what the emperors wanted the people of the empire to know of their accomplishments in war and peace.

From about 350 A.D., the brief time of Vetranio, the coinage shows who the emperor is and what his link is to Christianity. From the reign of Anastasius (491 A.D.) the gold and silver is totally Christian, while the bronze coinage tells everything about itself: the emperor who issued it, the denomination, the date of its issue, the city where it was struck, and even the working teams that made it. Few other things bring us such a diverse wealth of information over a 2,100-year period. The really surprising part is that ancient coins, compared to other forms of art, are very affordable, with prices starting at a dollar or two and many wonderful coins available for $5,000 or less.

Since ancient coins represent the origin of everyone who is from Europe, the Middle East, and North Africa, they have practically the same value in any country where the descendants of these people live, whether it is Chicago, Zurich, London, Paris, Munich, or Madrid.

Coins have been collected almost since they were issued. There is evidence that the leaders of some great cities issued wonderful artistic coins made by recognized artists so that future generations would know what heights they reached. During the civil war following the death of Nero in 68 A.D., coins from 70 years earlier were reissued in a revised style to reflect the multiple political positions that existed. During the reign of Trajan, coins from Julius Caesar, Titus, Vespasian, and others were reissued in commemoration. Mark Antony's legionary denarius was commemorated by Marcus Aurelius and Lucius Verus, who reissued it with their names.

Renaissance kings and princes collected coins, as evidenced by the work of the 16th-century forger Giovanni Cavino in Padua, Italy, who created sestertii of the most desired types, even a sestertius of Otho (69 A.D.), who never issued one. Also in the 16th century, the Gonzaga family stamped an eagle mark on every coin in their collection.

The bronze lepta popularly known as the "Widow's Mite" is just one example of an ancient coin that is inexpensive to acquire but rich in historical associations. (Actual size approx. 28 mm)

From the later 18th century to the early 20th century, there were many gentleman collectors. Apostolo Zeno (1668–1750), an Italian musician at the court of Austria's Maria Theresa, collected Roman coins. Also in Austria, the Trau family (Carl [1811–1887], Franz [1842–1905], and his son Franz [1881–1931]), who had the tea monopoly in Austria, amassed an amazingly complete collection of Roman coins, which was sold in 1935. Financier J.P. Morgan collected everything, including Greek and Roman coins, as did M.R. Jameson, a Scottish banker who lived in Paris. Jameson's collection was published in 1913 in Paris. Famed opera singer Enrico Caruso formed and sold at auction a collection of Roman aurei. George Gillette, whose family owned the chemical company Rhône-Poulenc, amassed a wonderful collection of Greek coins, which was sold after his death at a 1974 auction in Zurich. Giovanni Dattari, an Italian businessman living in Egypt during the 19th century, formed the best and most complete collection ever assembled of the Roman tetradrachms struck at Alexandria, and it was published in Cairo in 1901.

One of the most amazing collections of Greek coins was formed by Calouste Gulbenkian with the advice of E.S.G. Robinson of the British Museum. In an agreement with the Turkish Petroleum Company, Gulbenkian received 5% of all the oil revenues from the Middle East from 1928 until his death in 1955. He collected everything, including Greek coins, which now reside at the Gulbenkian Institute in Lisbon, Portugal, but are available to us in the form of a wonderfully printed two-volume set of books.

One of my favorite personalities is Dr. Samuel Pozzi, who was shot dead by a medical patient in 1918 for refusing to perform an unneeded operation. The sale of his coins in 1921 in Geneva started Jacob Hirsch in his series of earth-shattering sales using the name Ars Classica, which ran until 1938. There are many more, such as Richard Cyril Lockett, Sir Herman Weber, H.P. Hall—far too many to list them all. The Lockett and Weber collections are published, and there is an excellent auction catalog of the Hall sale from 1950. The important Hunt collection and the sales catalogs by Sotheby's from the early 1990s are good reference works that illustrate a vast range of coins.

Today ancient coins are collected around the globe. The main difference between collectors in the United States and Europe is that Europeans tend to keep their coins for generations, while Americans generally keep collections only 10 to 15 years on average. The Europeans have the right idea. After World War II the European collectors had all the knowledge and the Americans virtually none; now we are equal, but Europe probably has more collectors.

Prominent among early 20th-century collectors of ancient coins were such distinguished figures as (from left to right) Samuel Pozzi, Calouste Gulbenkian, and John Pierpont Morgan.

Should you decide to collect ancient coins, buy what appeals to you, unless you have decided in advance in which direction you want to go. Look at Greek, Roman, and Byzantine coins in all metals and find what attracts you most. You should subscribe to as many dealers' publications as you feel comfortable with and start to build a numismatic library. Your local library, with few exceptions, will have next to nothing, but most dealers in ancient coins also deal in numismatic books. Currently, George Kolbe, Charles Davis, John Burns, Spink, and Douglas Saville are noteworthy dealers in numismatic books.

When you start buying (unless you've met a dealer you already like), deal with a number of established firms, but then make a decision and do most of your business through the dealer you feel most comfortable with and who is most helpful to you. If you spend most of your money through one dealer you will become more important to that dealer and command more of his or her time. The dealer you choose should be able to give you advice on coins you are anticipating purchasing even from other dealers. If the dealer you choose tells you that everyone else's coins are inferior to his, pick another dealer. This dealer is serving himself more than you.

Another decision you must make while you are collecting ancient coins, unless you have an unlimited budget, is whether you want to have a lot of coins of lower quality or fewer coins of very high quality. If you want a lot of coins and enjoy that, that's fine, but do not expect to get more than a small fraction of what you paid for the coins when you decide to sell. Collectors and dealers alike have plenty of ordinary coins; not everyone has many extraordinary coins. If you buy the highest quality available, when you exit numismatics—if you have been collecting for 20 or more years—you should do well financially. People who build a logical collection, such as portraits of all Roman emperors, all the types of Syracusan tetradrachms, the coins of Alexander the Great, or all the coins of the Severan dynasty, for example, usually do quite well at point of sale. Never, however, start collecting ancient coins to make money. Do it because you love it.

Buy as many books as you can and learn as much as you can. Knowledge is not only power, but excitement. When you learn why a coin was struck, who struck it, or under what circumstances, it can make the coin more of a treasure to you. If there are coin shows in your area you should attend, meet the dealers in person, and look at as many coins at the show as you possibly can. The more coins you see, the more you will know.

One of the best numismatic organizations to join is the American Numismatic Society in New York City. The ANS has a museum that owns one of the finest collections of ancient coins in existence. It also issues an excellent scholarly journal as well as numerous new publications. You can also join the Royal Numismatic Society at the British Museum or at least purchase their excellent publication *Numismatic Chronicle* from Spink. Do try to buy back issues of both ANS journals and the *Numismatic Chronicle*. The American Numismatic Association is an excellent collector organization based in Colorado Springs, but its main thrust is American coins. Most large cities have ancient coin clubs; it is worthwhile to join, meet other collectors, and discuss your newest acquisitions and show them to fellow collectors.

GRADING AND AUTHENTICATING ANCIENT COINS

Grading ancient coins is virtually the same as grading American coins. The primary difference is that most American coins are perfectly struck, whereas most ancient coins are imperfectly struck. A double-struck American coin can be extremely valuable, but a double-struck ancient coin, whose intended design has been destroyed, can be nearly worthless. A Mint State or Uncirculated coin has unbroken luster. There are a few exceptions, such as the Jewish shekels of the First Revolt, which are struck in such high relief that the highest points of the coin never came into contact with the die; thus, these coins have no luster in those areas. In general, however, you must remember that the key is *unbroken* luster, as an ancient coin can be Mint State but poorly struck. Often this

The reverses of Philip II tetradrachms struck at different times show the dramatic deterioration in artistic quality that took place in posthumous issues. (Actual size approx. 25 mm)

is the case when worn dies were used to produce the coin. A well-struck Mint State ancient coin is worth far more than a weakly struck Mint State ancient coin. An Extremely Fine coin is one that has most of the detail intact, but not all of the luster. A Very Fine coin is one with substantial wear but a decent amount of detail remaining. A Fine coin is a rather worn coin with profiles clear but not much detail remaining. The condition of a coin, as far as the amount of wear, can be less important than its artistic quality. For example, a Philip II tetradrachm of very high style has on the reverse a large, proud, muscular horse with a tiny jockey. The later issues of the same coin have a small, almost doglike horse with a very large jockey, and are far less desirable. This is an extreme example, but one that is very illustrative.

Centering is also very important on an ancient coin. A tetradrachm of Athens bears the helmeted head of Athena with a crest extending from the front to the back of the helmet. A perfectly centered Athenian tetradrachm that shows the full crest and the full face and neck of Athena can be worth $5,000 in Mint State. A Mint State tetradrachm with the head of Athena and no crest or partial crest may be worth $3,500. A coin with the back of the helmet off flan may be worth $3,000. A coin with Athena's nose and lips off center may be worth $500. Again, this is an extreme example, and these values are not absolute. Variations can occur when the head of Athena lacks the crest but is well centered, with very high relief and extremely beautiful art, and thus can be worth more than a perfectly centered Athena with a full crest that is artistically poor or has a large die break that obliterates Athena's eye. The sophistication required for such judgments will come to you with experience; it comes faster when you have a good teacher (e.g., an excellent dealer to work with).

Any time something of value exists, there will also be a fake version of it. Fake ancient coins were created in ancient times and are now considered contemporary copies or ancient forgeries. From the moment coins were created, fourrées were made. These are coins, some official, some not, that usually have a silver coating over a copper core but were passed as full-silver coins. The Celtic copies of the coins of Philip II were minted in France, England, Germany, and even farther east and attempted to resemble familiar Macedonian coins. While these coins were fakes to the Macedonians, they had the correct weight of silver and are now considered legitimate Celtic coinage of the period. Cavino in Padua, Italy, created wonderful sestertii that copied ancient coins but were in fact made in the Renaissance. Although they are fakes they are still collectable as artistic pieces from the Renaissance. German counterfeiter Carl Wilhelm Becker made fake silver coins in the early 1800s that were sold as genuine. They are still fakes, but are collected as the work of a famous 19th-century forger.

The easiest way to make a forgery is to make a cast of an ancient coin. Casts never have the sharpness of a die-struck coin and the weight is frequently wrong. When forgers use a die that

Variations in centering, relief, and die condition can greatly affect the aesthetic value and desirability of Athens coinage, as seen here.

they have cut themselves, invariably they make an error in the way the die is cut, so any knowledgeable collector will immediately feel that something is wrong. New die-struck forgeries are struck on metal that looks too new. It is very difficult to put this quality into words, but when you see a fake alongside an original you will be able to tell the difference. If you travel to Greece or Italy and a nine-year-old walks up to you with a "great bargain" on an ancient coin, remember that unless God brings you coffee in the morning you are not so blessed. If you think the nine-year-old child is a sucker for selling you a great coin so cheaply, look in the mirror and you'll find the fool. Coins or antiquities sold to tourists in Italy, Greece, Egypt, Israel, or anywhere that archeology sites and tourists come together are almost never genuine. The best protection against getting stuck with a forgery is to buy only from legitimate dealers who unconditionally guarantee the authenticity of what they sell.

Although there are many reference books on ancient coins—the library at my company contains 16,500 volumes—no single work exists that covers all ancient coins in depth. The best general reference for Greek coins is the British Museum's *Catalogue of Greek Coins*, which consists of 29 volumes. For Roman coins, *Roman Imperial Coins* and *British Museum Coins* are excellent, thorough references. The eight-volume set *Description historique des monnaies frappées sous l'Empire Romain* by Henry Cohen, written in 1857 (in French), is also first class; it contains values in French gold francs. You do not need to know French to use the Cohen reference, however, because the coins are listed by emperor and arranged alphabetically according to reverse inscriptions. The reprint of Cohen's set comes with a small multilingual dictionary. Great references for Roman Republic coins were written by E.A. Sydenham and Michael Crawford and are (like the Cohen work) known by the last names of the authors. For Byzantine coins, the Dumbarton Oaks catalogs are an excellent reference. When you become a more focused collector, there are specialized books in many areas of numismatics, such as *Syracusan Decadrachms of Euainetos*, written by Albert Gallatin in 1930; *Temple Coins of Olympia*, on ancient Olympic coins, by Charles T. Seltman, published in 1921; and *Coins of Alexander the Great and Philip Arrhidaeus*, by Martin Price, from 1991. For Byzantine coins, an excellent specialized work is *Moneta Imperii Byzantini* by Wolfgang Hahn, first published in Vienna in 1973, although it only covers the period up to Leo III, ending in 741 A.D. Among the least expensive references are the books published by Spink and currently authored by David Sear. These handbooks list many coins in every area of ancient numismatics, but the coin prices—which are quoted in English pounds—are not perfect, as they tend to be too high on the common coins and too low on the rare coins.

Another way to build up a modest reference library is to save auction catalogs and price lists. You must keep in mind, however, that these are sales tools written not only to inform but also to persuade the reader to make a purchase. The other drawback to a reference library of only auction catalogs and price lists is that they will quote information from other volumes, but if you do not have those references you cannot tell if the information has been skewed.

There is no question that the best library is made up of standard reference books, auction catalogs, price lists, and scholarly works published by museums and serious numismatic organizations, which every country has.

The Internet is a great way to find many real coins—and frequently even more fake coins than anywhere else. You should not venture into either outer space or cyberspace without being thoroughly prepared. There are many individuals floating in cyberspace who want only one thing: your money. Don't go swimming with sharks unless you are well protected. A long list of positive responses from past customers does not mean that your cyberdealer is honest. There are, of course, many good dealers on the Internet and some very good ways to find them. VCoins.com and sixbid.com are excellent Web sites and may help you if you have problems with a coin purchased through their member dealers. Some other online venues are not as helpful.

My last words are these: learn as much as you can about the area of ancient coins you plan to collect, and have a strong relationship with a very good dealer of your choosing whom you are constantly testing. As a dealer who has been in the business for more than 40 years, I can tell you that a really focused collector will know as much as, and sometimes more than, a very good dealer in the collector's chosen area of specialization. Be that collector!

A NOTE ON PRICING

The market values given for each coin in this book are often the prices realized (at auction or private sale) for particular specimens. It is difficult, if not impossible, to place values on ancient coins as *types*—to say, for example, that "this general type is worth $X in Very Fine and $Z in Extremely Fine." For discerning collectors, variations in planchet quality, strike, centering, and other aesthetic factors, as well as differences in die engraver, mint, and other production variations, can greatly affect an ancient coin's value. The prices given herein for specific examples can be used to extrapolate general values or ranges, but they are not guaranteed values for each type.

IONIA ELECTRUM STATER

GREECE · CIRCA 650 B.C.

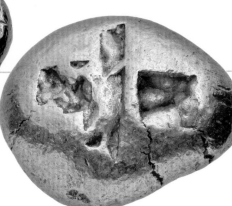

Actual size approx. 20 mm

One of the early appearances of these coins in recent times was the October 1987 sale of the Rosen collection, where one brought 18,000 Swiss francs (SFr). When these come to market now they usually bring $20,000 to $25,000, and they normally are in Mint State.

With this coin, we stand at the very beginning of coinage—at the birth of the very first object that can be called a true coin. The date of its emergence remains disputed, but most authorities agree that 650 B.C. is a reasonable approximation. Civilizations had existed in Egypt and Mesopotamia long before that time, but those societies had functioned without coinage. In their rigid, hierarchical governance systems, the state controlled most large transfers of goods, while barter or weighing of metal sufficed for the minor transactions of individuals.

> With this, we stand at the birth of the very first object that can be called a true coin.

The Lydian and Greek societies, however, were much less restrictive. Individuals, rather than the state, controlled trade, and that sort of commerce required a ready and reliable medium of exchange. Unmarked, irregular lumps of metal were inconvenient because they had to be weighed and their purity determined with every transaction. At some point circa 650 B.C., a system of standardized weights was developed and lumps of standard weight began to appear.

The standardized coins were so successful and evolved so rapidly that they soon carried more complex obverse designs that made them easier to recognize and showed them to be products of reliable authorities. Before long reverse types began to appear, replacing the old incuse punch marks. We do not know whether governments or individuals issued these first coins, but governments soon monopolized their production and all the various processes that developed to support it.

The earliest coins were made of electrum, a naturally occurring alloy of gold and silver. Eventually coins of pure silver and, occasionally, pure gold replaced electrum at most mints. The stater stood at the top of the denominational chain, followed by the 1/2 stater, 1/3 stater, 1/6, 1/12, and so forth, all the way to a tiny but still highly valuable 1/96 stater coin. The first pieces were typeless, meaning that they had a plain, featureless obverse and a simple punch on the reverse. Soon after—if not at the same time—rough striations and punch marks, such as those on this Ionia stater, were added. The reverse began to evolve as well, moving quickly beyond the three distinct incuse punches seen here. Within the next hundred years, local mints began putting images on their coins, which as time went on became more elaborate and artistic, finally evolving into the now familiar sociopolitical representations and portraiture.

Actual sizes approx. 22 mm (top) and 15 mm

With an appearance in Munich at Gorny and Mosch in 2007, it is very difficult to gauge the value of this extremely rare issue. In 1973 this coin would have been worth $100,000, but in 2000 at the Tkalec sale of February 29, lot 114 brought SFr 280,000 (about $165,000). There are only three inscribed staters and four 1/3 staters (trites). The trite at left is unique due to the left-facing stag and the swastika beneath it.

The city of Ephesus lies on the alluvial plain of the lower Cayster. No one is sure when it was first settled, but archeological remains found there date from at least the Mycenaean period, circa 1300 B.C., and there may have been an even more ancient native settlement on the site. It is not known whether the Mycenaean Greek town survived the years between 1200 and 800 B.C. (known as the Greek Dark Ages because no written records and relatively little information exist for that period), or whether the Mycenaean settlement died out and the site was resettled by later Greek colonists. In any case, the city eventually prospered and became a meeting place for Greeks and native Anatolians, as well as for merchants and traders from the exotic ports of Syria and Egypt. Because they lived in a center of commerce, the people of Ephesus were attracted to coinage, the new invention that made buying and selling—not to mention saving profits—so much easier. It was at Ephesus that the first coin bearing an inscription was struck.

The obverse of this early electrum stater shows a stag grazing right, and a Greek legend above that translates to "I Am the Badge of Phanes." The reverse bears three punch marks from the metal driven into the obverse die. Though the grazing stag may have been his badge, Phanes himself remains unknown to us, but he was probably an aristocrat or powerful merchant who lived around 600 B.C. However, the stag was also the sacred animal of Artemis, the chief goddess at Ephesus. For a long time, the Phanes stater was

thought to be unique, but in recent years new discoveries have produced at least one more stater, a number of trites (1/3 staters) bearing only a stag and Phanes' name, and 1/6, 1/12, 1/24, 1/48, and 1/96 fractions of the stater with only the forepart of a stag and no legend at all. (The 1/96 is a very tiny coin indeed.) Even though we know next to nothing about Phanes and the circumstances surrounding the minting of this coin, we have here the first coin with an inscription, representing a marked development beyond the earlier, more primitive coins, which had only simple types such as striated lines.

> It was at Ephesus that the first coin bearing an inscription was struck.

Ephesus went on to become one of the most prosperous and famous cities in the ancient world, a center of art, architecture, and extravagance. Its magnificent central temple, dedicated to Artemis of Ephesus, was one of the Seven Wonders of the Ancient World, and the cult of Artemis (or Diana, to use her Roman name) of Ephesus remained so important that support for the goddess provoked a near riot when St. Paul tried to preach in the city about 650 years after this coin was issued.

POSEIDONIA STATER

GREECE · CIRCA 530–500 B.C.

Actual size approx. 30 mm

In the 1960s and 1970s these coins varied between $2,000 and $12,000. Values range widely because of the many different styles and qualities, as well as the fact that these coins, being very thin, frequently crystallize and break. Today an Extremely Fine coin of good style would bring about $30,000.

The city of Poseidonia began as a Greek colony established in southern Italy by settlers from nearby Sybaris, a city famous for its wealth and luxury. It was named for its chief deity, Poseidon the sea god, and soon grew prosperous. It seems likely that the image of Poseidon on the coins reproduces the cult statue of the god in the city's chief temple.

The coins of Poseidonia are particularly treasured for their fine artistry. The figure of Poseidon is finely detailed and beautifully proportioned.

This stater belongs to a group of early strikings from the Greek cities of Poseidonia, Croton, Sybaris, Metapontum, Caulonia, Tarentum, Laus, Siris, and Pyxus—all in southern Italy. They are distinguished by their broad, thin flans and the unusual technique of repeating the obverse type in incuse on the reverse. Some of the other cities produced coins on which the incuse reverse was sometimes quite different from the relief obverse.

The coins of Poseidonia are particularly treasured for their fine artistry. In this case, the obverse shows a standing figure of Poseidon, brandishing his trident and advancing to the right. The initial letters of the city's name appear in the left field, with an elaborate border surrounding. The reverse repeats the entire composition but in incuse rather than relief. The figure of Poseidon is executed in a vigorous Archaic style, finely detailed and beautifully proportioned. The engraver has not only depicted the individual muscles of the legs and abdomen, but has also included the design and tassels on the cloth mantle draped across Poseidon's shoulders, as well as the details of his highly ornamented trident. Unfortunately, later issues of the stater were not as elegant. By 480 B.C. the flans had become smaller and thicker, and the artistic quality of the Poseidon figure had markedly declined.

650 B.C.   450   250   50   50   250   450   650   850   1050   1250   1450 A.D.

Croesus was king of Lydia from 560 to 546 B.C., when he was defeated by King Darius I of Persia. He must have been an exceptional individual, since the Persians kept him as puppet king after his defeat. Evidently Croesus did not have the ego of his predecessors, such as Alyattes II, because unlike them Croesus never placed his name on his coinage.

When Croesus reigned, coinage was a relatively new invention, probably less than 100 years old. Until this time coins had been made from a natural mixture of gold and silver known as electrum. Croesus was not only the first to use pure gold and silver, but he created a complex interrelated, bimetallic monetary system. Silver and gold traded at a rate of 13:1. At the top of the coinage system were gold and silver staters of 10-plus grams; therefore, 13 silver staters equaled 1 gold stater. The coinage went all the way down to a gold 1/12 stater at .33 grams and a silver 1/24 stater at .36 grams. Although we illustrate one at .40 grams, in all probability scales were not accurate to a fraction of 1/3 of a gram.

Initially, Croesus experimented with his coinage, striking at least three trial coins. Here we illustrate three, two of which are struck from the same die. The most outstanding of these is the heavy gold stater (1), showing a leaping lion with a wart on his forehead facing a bull. The wart was on the lion's head on the trites, or 1/3 staters, issued by Croesus's predecessors, but it does not appear on any of the rest of Croesus's coinage. The wart is the transitional link that ties things together.

There are two prototype staters represented by three coins of 10-plus grams, with two from the same dies and one prototype light stater or siglos of 5-plus grams also struck from the same dies as the pair of 10-gram staters. Number 16 is unique, while the two others (17 and 18) share the die with the siglos (21). In all four cases the forepaw of the lion is raised, while the foreleg of the bull bends at the joint. The regular-issue heavy staters in gold (2) and silver (19 and 20) show the forepaw and foreleg of the lion and bull respectively extended straight forward, forming a base of sorts. All the rest of the denominations follow that format.

Most of the recorded 1/12 and 1/24 staters in gold and silver, and all of those illustrated, were struck with the same dies, which indicates that they were a very small issue, probably only for local use.

In 1977 an Extremely Fine heavy gold stater brought SFr 9,500 at Bank Leu. Today that coin would bring $17,500. An entire collection has never been offered publicly, but one sold privately for $120,000 and a few years later got an offer of $250,000, which was declined.

Actual sizes approx. 5-22 mm. All coins shown 1.75x actual size

Gold and silver coins being struck with the same dies was unheard of in the Greek world but was done by the Romans, who used gold dies to strike silver coins when the gold issue was completed.

Gold coins in this series were issued in heavy and light versions. When I first published an article about the coinage of Croesus in *The Celator* in 1990, I had recently acquired a heavy 1/24 stater (14) of .42 grams and wrote in the article that a light 1/24 must have existed. Sure enough, a few years later Sotheby's alerted me that a light 1/24 was coming up in one of their first online auctions; of course I purchased it, and it is illustrated (15) at .33 grams.

After the defeat of Croesus, the Persians scrapped his wonderful system for a two-coin issue. The coins are in gold (4) and in silver (22). The lion and the bull are larger and somewhat clumsy, unlike the delicate work of Croesus. There have been questions about whether Croesus or the Persians were responsible for this elaborate coinage. For me, and now most everyone else, there is no question. The Persians, after the cessation of the lion-and-bull type, issued a gold daric and silver siglos portraying what is called a kneeling-running king. A people who used two-denomination coinage as they did, and only for the Greeks they conquered, would never do what Croesus did. Until now, no one has explained what the lion-and-bull type could mean. For years, I, like many others, thought the lion stood for Lydia and the bull for someone they defeated. Finally I went back to basics and came to a different conclusion. The lion is the symbol of strength and power, while the bull represents fertility. The coin types tell us that the Lydians are representing that they are strong and fertile, which is very important and not a given—especially in the ancient world.

King Croesus of Lydia, even today renowned for his wealth, created the first bimetallic coinage. Illustrated here is a range of coins struck under his rule, as well as later Persian issues showing the deterioration of the lion-and-bull design.

Actual sizes approx. 25 mm (top) and 20 mm

In the 1970s these coins brought $8,000 in Fine and $20,000 in Extremely Fine. Today a Fine coin would bring the same, but an Extremely Fine would command $35,000. These coins frequently come worn and off-center, with centered Extremely Fine coins bringing a premium.

While the earliest Greek coins were made of the alloy electrum, most city-states abandoned that metal in favor of pure silver. Of the few that did not, the most notable was Cyzicus.

> When this long and varied series began, its one consistent symbol, the tunny, was the only image on the coin.

Located on the waterway connecting the Aegean to the Black Sea, Cyzicus was a rich trading city and the mother city to many of the Greek colonies on the coast of the Black Sea. It was there that Cyzicus's extensive coinage of electrum staters, struck from about 520 to about 340 B.C., circulated. These coins were always struck on thick flans, with a four-part incuse for the reverse. It appears that Cyzicus issued a different obverse type each year. The tunny or tuna fish, the badge of the city, was rarely used as the main type, but was always present as an adjunct symbol. More than 180 types of staters are recorded—even more for the smaller 1/6 staters known as *hektes*.

When this long and varied series began, its one consistent symbol, the tunny, was the only image on the coin. One early stater shows a winged or flying tunny. There followed a long period of time when both mythological and real animals appeared with a tunny fish, which is usually at the bottom of the coin. The next series of images portrayed humans—both real and mythological—and always with the tunny at the bottom. Sometimes the figures rest on the fish; more rarely, they hold it by the tail. One late type is thought to be a portrait of Philip II, king of Macedonia and father of Alexander the Great.

Illustrated here are examples portraying a real beast, a bull (above), and a mythological beast-woman, a sphinx (below).

ALEXANDER I OF MACEDONIA OCTODRACHM

GREECE · 492–480 B.C.

Actual size approx. 36 mm

In the 1960s these coins were bringing SFr 12,000; in the May 28, 1974, "Kunstfreundes" sale by Bank Leu and Münzen und Medaillen, at the height of the '70s boom, one brought SFr 54,000. In recent years a number of these coins have come to market, so at the moment they are bringing $20,000, but when the supply is absorbed they will go up in price.

Macedonia is an area now in northern Greece; in ancient times, it was a separate land. Although greatly influenced by the culture of Greece, the Macedonians, who spoke a different language, lagged behind the Greeks in most areas. Macedonia was surrounded by still more barbarous tribes, with whom there was frequent war, and colonies established by the Greeks cut off the Macedonians from their own coast. Moreover, the Macedonian nobility were a quarrelsome, violent group, often at war with one another and united only in opposition to the growth of a strong national monarchy.

> Alexander I struck the bold octodrachm, almost certainly issued as payment to the Persians.

Nevertheless, shortly around 500 B.C., such a Macedonian monarchy was beginning to emerge and unite the land. Then a new power, Persia, emerged on the scene. In 492 B.C., the Persians established military domination in the area, and Alexander I had no choice but to cooperate and pay tribute—even as he sought to maintain as much autonomy as possible.

It was during this time that Alexander I struck the bold octodrachm, almost certainly issued as payment to the Persians. The obverse shows a horseman holding two spears and standing beside his steed. The subject and ripe Archaic style relate to the tribal coinages of groups such as the Edones and Bisaltai, to whom this octodrachm was earlier attributed. Alexander's later issues, bearing his name, have a more developed style but lack the primitive vigor of the earlier issues. The reverse is a simple, textured square incuse divided into quarters. Most likely, no more than 50 of these impressive coins are recorded.

SYRACUSE ALPHEIOS FACING HEAD TETRADRACHM

GREECE · CIRCA 485 B.C.

Actual size approx. 27 mm

This coin is the only one recorded, and as it has never come up for sale it is difficult to value, but it is no doubt worth in excess of $100,000.

This fabulous coin, known from a single example, was struck by the tyrant Gelon after he captured the city of Syracuse in 485 B.C., and fills a previous void in the chronology of this mint's coinage. The coinage of Syracuse in Sicily is among the best studied and most admired, for it is of remarkable beauty and artistic style.

The style of the obverse detail is a tour de force of ancient art.

The river god on the obverse is among the earliest facing heads known on any ancient coin, an exceedingly rare occurrence during the Archaic period. Facing heads were previously known on very few coin types, such as the Wappenmünzen of Athens and staters of Neapolis, both of which show facing gorgons. This coin offers the oldest representation in Greek art of the local river god Alpheios, who was known in human form only from the east pediment of the temple of Zeus in Olympia. As the lyric poet Pindar recounts, Alpheios was a hunter who fell in love with the huntress nymph Arethusa. Arethusa fled his advances and transformed into a spring, whereupon Alpheios became a river and mingled his waters with hers. This legend is closely associated with the foun-

dation of Syracuse. At one time it was thought that the coin depicted Acheloös, a different river god of Greek myth, but the recent study by Carmen Arnold-Biucchi and Arnold-Peter Weiss (2007) has identified the figure as Alpheios.

The obverse shows a facing male head with a long beard, which is rendered in long wavy and parallel strands in relief; the hair above the forehead is rendered in a similar way. Two horns and nonhuman ears are visible. Eyebrows and pupils are rendered by relief contours, and the pupils and irises are clearly marked too. The face is distinguished by a strong, straight nose and round fleshy cheeks, and a moustache frames the finely engraved lips. On the reverse, two large barley grains in relief parallel each other in a deep incuse square. They possibly represent the denomination of a tetradrachm, since the standard early issues of Syracuse were didrachms (one barley grain per didrachm). To the left, facing downward from top to bottom, is the legend ΣVRA. The style of the obverse detail is a tour de force of ancient art, especially considering that it precedes by many years the famous profile heads of the Aetna Master.

650 B.C.   450   250   50   50   250   450   650   850   1050   1250   1450 A.D.

DELPHIC TRIDRACHM

GREECE · CIRCA 479 B.C.

Actual size approx. 23 mm

These coins are very important and rare, but the supply was improved when seven specimens emerged in the Asyut hoard of 1969. In 1979 one of these very coins brought SFr 58,000. At LHS Numismatik in Zurich in 2001 one of these brought SFr 225,000, which was thought to be a very high price.

Delphi is located in central Greece in the mountains north of the Gulf of Corinth, which almost cuts Greece in half. It was not a city, but rather a fairly small town. Here, though, stood the Temple of Apollo—one of the most important and richest temples of the ancient world—and its famous oracle.

Long before the Greeks arrived in this part of the world, Delphi was already a shrine to the earth fertility goddess Gaia, and her totem, the python, who carried prayers to her deep underground. According to legend, Apollo killed the serpent, but memorialized it by naming his priestess the Pythia. It was the Pythia who brought worshippers' inquiries to Apollo and provided his oracular responses. The oracle gave advice to all who came—kings, nobles, and private individuals, Greeks and non-Greeks alike.

According to the myth, the Pythia sat in a chamber deep inside the temple. There she inhaled hypnotic vapors rising from a cleft in the rock. The vapors induced a trancelike state through which she was able to communicate with the oracle. The ancient author Diodorus wrote that this phenomenon was discovered when some goats feeding near a chasm in the rocks became intoxicated by fumes emitting from the opening. The strange antics of the goats caught the attention of the herdsman and led him to the spot where the temple was built.

Offerings made to Apollo by kings or cities were kept in a special treasury display, but those of private individuals accumulated in the temple itself. While the town of Delphi did not normally issue coins, these gifts of private individuals may have been converted into coins shortly before 490 B.C. to finance building activity at the temple.

The Delphic tridrachm is part of an issue struck shortly before Darius of Persia invaded Greece in 479 B.C.

The Delphic tridrachm is part of an issue struck shortly after the Greeks defeated Xerxes and his Persian forces in 479 B.C. The coin's obverse depicts two ram-headed rhytons side by side. These ceremonial vessels, used to pour out offerings of wine to Apollo, were booty seized from the Persians; imitations were later created by Greek artists. The ram's head on the rhytons symbolizes Apollo in his role as the god of domestic flocks and herds. Above the rhytons are two dolphins leaping, and the name of the city surrounds the design. The dolphins call to mind Apollo's special cult name, "Apollo Delphinos," as well as the name of the town.

The reverse resembles a coffered ceiling, divided into four deep squares, each containing a dolphin and a palmette. This design may replicate the actual ceiling of the temple at Delphi itself.

AETNA TETRADRACHM

Actual size approx. 26 mm

This coin has never sold. It resides in the collection of the Royal Library of Belgium. If one did come up for sale, it might bring $2,500,000 or more.

Syracuse, located on the eastern coast of Sicily, was the largest and most important Greek city on the island. When the Sicilian Greeks were threatened by the Carthaginians (who controlled the western half of Sicily), they typically united under the guidance of a strong leader whose basis of power depended upon control of Syracuse. Later, when the Carthaginian danger had passed, these leaders encountered problems as the other Greek cities of Sicily attempted to free themselves from their domination.

> The coin is one of the best examples of the severe style of Greek art, representing the transition between the stiffer Archaic and the more naturalistic classical styles.

This was the situation in 476 B.C. Hieron, the tyrant of Syracuse, had recently defeated Carthage. He then resorted to violent measures to control the Sicilian Greeks who, with the danger of Carthaginian attack removed, turned against his authority. The city of Catania, located in eastern Sicily near Syracuse at the foot of the active volcano Mt. Aetna, posed a particular threat to Hieron. He expelled the native population and renamed the city Aetna, resettling it with immigrants from Syracuse and the Peloponnesus in Greece.

Shortly after this the city struck its first coins, a splendid issue of tetradrachms today known from one surviving specimen. The coin's obverse features the magnificent head of Silenus, wearing an ivy wreath. Silenus was the leader of the mythological satyrs and was the constant companion of Dionysus, god of wine. (Today, the town—once again called Catania—remains famous for its wines.) Around the head of Silenus the name of the city is spelled out. Below, we find a beetle, which may represent the artist's signature, perhaps in the form of a pun on his name. The reverse shows Zeus seated on a throne covered by a lion skin. He holds a thunderbolt and a staff, while before him an eagle perches on a pine tree.

The coin is one of the best examples of the severe style of Greek art, representing the transition between the stiffer Archaic and the more naturalistic classical styles. The relief is extraordinarily high, the detail amazing, and the composition original. It stands alone as a monument of Greek coinage.

650 B.C.   450   250   50   50   250   450   650   850   1050   1250   1450 A.D.

COS DISCUS THROWER STATER

GREECE · CIRCA 470–450 B.C.

Actual size approx. 21 mm

There has been no new find of these coins in over 50 years, which has increased the desire of collectors to own one. The price, strangely, has remained within the SFr 24,000 to 42,000 range. The condition of these coins is consistent, in the Fine to Very Fine range, which would suggest that they all come from one late 19th-century find.

Cos is an island near the southwestern coast of what is now Turkey. It was colonized by Greeks as early as the 11th century B.C. and became a center for the worship of the god Apollo and his son, Asklepios, the god of healing. Cos was part of the Dorian Pentapolis, an alliance of five neighboring cities founded by Greeks from the southern part of Greece.

This extraordinary issue of silver staters was struck to celebrate athletic games held in honor of Apollo.

The earliest coins of Cos simply showed a crab, the symbol of the island city, on the obverse and a rough incuse square on the reverse. After a long interval during which the city issued no coins, Cos produced a new coinage circa 470 to 450 B.C. This extraordinary issue of silver staters was struck to celebrate athletic games held in honor of Apollo. Athletes from all five member cities of the Dorian Pentapolis took part in these games. The first-place winners received bronze tripods, which they then dedicated to Apollo.

On the obverse, these new staters depict a young man in the first stage of throwing the discus. The youthful thrower is shown in a dynamic pose typical of the high classical style and probably reflects to some degree the famous statue of a discus thrower created only a few years earlier by the artist Myron. The original of Myron's sculpture is lost, but copies have survived. Like it, the coin is composed of a series of carefully balanced triangles, an artful composition that nevertheless manages to be naturalistic and captures what the Greeks called "symmetria," or natural balance. It is not known why the citizens of Cos chose the discus thrower to symbolize the games; perhaps a local citizen had won that competition. To the left of the discus thrower stands a tripod (the victors' prize), and to the right is the name of the city. On the reverse, a crab, the city's badge, sits in a shallow incuse in a striated field.

Only about 30 examples exist today of what is universally recognized as one of the most innovative and artistically important Greek coins.

SYRACUSE DEMARETEION DECADRACHM

GREECE · CIRCA 470 B.C.

Actual size approx. 35 mm

As early as 1948 a worn example in only Fine brought SFr 20,000, and in 1979 a Very Fine example brought SFr 125,000. If an Extremely Fine specimen came up today it would easily surpass $500,000.

The city of Syracuse was the largest, most prosperous Greek settlement on the isle of Sicily. There was a complex relationship between Syracuse and the other Greek cities on the island, as well as between the Greeks as a whole and Carthage, the Punic city in North Africa that dominated Sicily's western half. During times of peace with Carthage, the Greek cities in Sicily tended to function independently of one another, sometimes to the point of hostility, but whenever Carthage threatened to conquer the entire island, the Greeks would unite behind whatever tyrant controlled Syracuse at the time. Once the unified Greeks had defeated Carthage, they would return to their various cities, revert to their quarrelsome independence, and begin the cycle all over again.

When the Sicilian Greeks defeated Carthage in its 480 B.C. bid to conquer Sicily, Demarete, wife of Gelon, then tyrant of Syracuse, begged her husband to grant generous terms to the Carthaginians. (Many had been captured, and it seemed Carthage might even lose its long-held western portion of Sicily.) The grateful Carthaginians sent her a golden crown in appreciation of her appeal. It is traditionally believed that she sold the crown for the silver used to strike these magnificent decadrachms. There is a problem, however, with this delightful story. The Carthaginians probably sent the crown to Demarete around 480 B.C., but art historians and numismatists maintain that the decadrachms were struck about a decade later, around 470. Moreover, the iconography of the coin does not refer to Demarete in any clear fashion, but appears instead to celebrate the chariot victories of Hieron,

Gelon's brother and successor, in the Pythian Games at Delphi in 470 B.C. and the Olympics in 468. Whatever the reason for the striking of these impressive coins, they are one of the greatest monuments of Greek art of the fifth century B.C.

While the coin's composition still owes much to Archaic Greek art, it also reflects the beginning of the transition to the more naturalistic early classical style. The obverse features a quadriga (four-horse chariot) driven by a charioteer while the goddess Nike flies above, ready to crown the horses with a laurel wreath. A lion, possibly the symbol of Demarete's family, occupies the exergue. On the reverse, a head of the nymph Arethusa is surrounded by four dolphins symbolizing the island of Ortygia on which the city of Syracuse had been originally founded. (The city soon outgrew Ortygia and was moved to the larger island of Sicily.) Arethusa's hair is a carefully designed, complex arrangement of patterned parallel lines that lend grace and formality to the portrait. The head still exhibits the Archaic facing eye, although the first signs of its evolution into a more natural profile eye are evident in its more refined shape (not a simple oval) and its slight opening at the inner corner. This blending of the Archaic imposition of artificial order and pattern with nascent classical naturalism and idealism has produced a work of memorable beauty. The distinctive features of the nymph have led many to imagine that the head is actually a portrait of Queen Demarete, but proof is lacking, and the date of the coin places its creation well before portraits of living individuals, rather than gods, are known to have appeared on coins.

650 B.C.   450   250   50   50   250   450   650   850   1050   1250   1450 A.D.

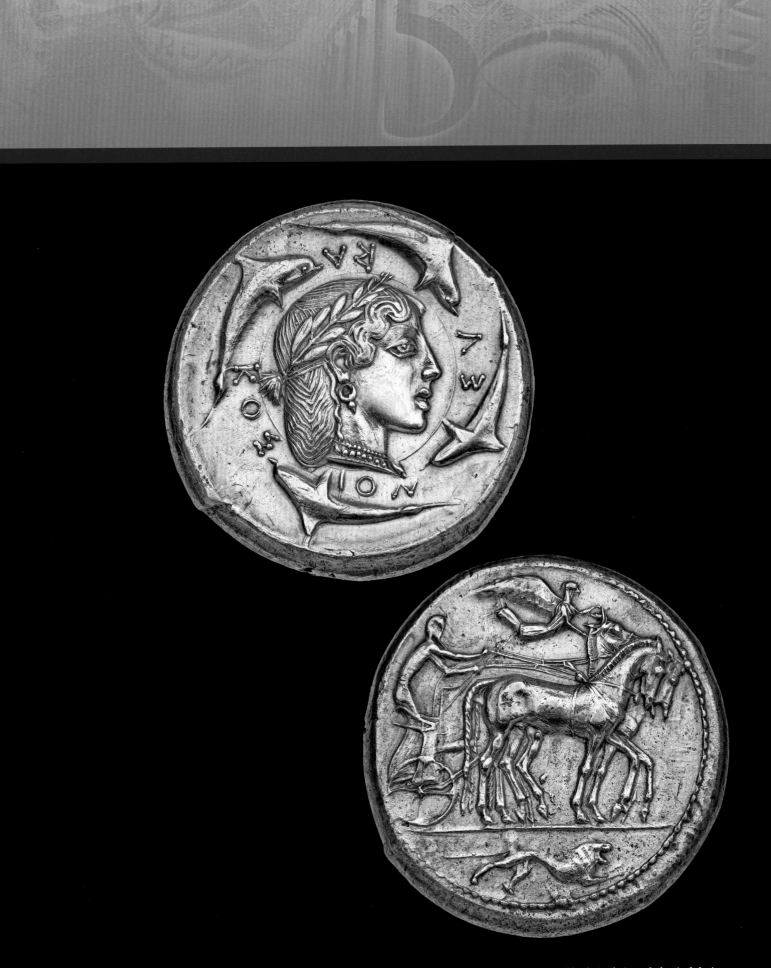

The decadrachm associated with Queen Demarete beautifully synthesizes elements of both Archaic and classical design to become one of the finest achievements of fifth-century Greek art.

Actual size approx. 33 mm

The population of these coins has tripled since 1970, when Chester Starr recorded 13 coins. In 1968 a Very Fine example brought SFr 95,000, but in 1974, before the hoards came out, the finest known example brought SFr 820,000. Today these magnificent coins bring $325,000.

Athens, located in the heart of the Attica region of Greece, prospered in the fertile plain between the Ilissos and Eridanos rivers. The proximity to the rivers and the port at Piraeus on the Aegean Sea helped Athens grow into a dominant political and economic force in the ancient Greek world.

Though Athens is famous for the consistent quality of its coinage, in both imagery and standard weights, its decadrachm is unlike any other Athenian coin. It weighs approximately 43 grams, which fills the hand and makes a weighty impression. On the obverse, the high-relief, helmeted head of Athena is in Archaic style, recalling the art of an earlier century. The reverse appears to be more contemporary, showing the facing owl with wings spread threateningly, as if protecting its nest—that nest being Athens itself. In the upper left corner of the reverse there is an olive sprig, and on the obverse, three olive leaves decorate Athena's helmet. Olive oil was a major export of the region, and according to myth, it was Athena who created the first olive tree as a gift to the Athenians.

Previously thought to have been issued in connection with the battle of Marathon in 490 B.C., the decadrachm is now recognized to have been struck several decades later, about 465 B.C. At that time, Pericles, leader of the Athenian democracy, had just achieved political dominance in Athens, and war had been declared against the Persians. Specimens of this important coin are known to have been found in Anatolia and Syria, indicating that the issue probably served as a war subsidy for Athens's allies. When Chester G. Starr wrote his 1970 book *Athenian Coinage 480–449 B.C.*, only 13 recorded specimens of the Athenian decadrachm were known to exist. The population of this coin is now closer to 40, of which more than half are in museums.

The owl's wings are spread threateningly, protecting its nest—Athens itself.

Greek decadrachms were often commemorative, and scholars have been attempting to connect the issuance of the Athenian decadrachm with a specific historic event. The early Marathon theory gave way to a later connection to the battles of Salamis and Plataea in 480 or 479 B.C. However, even Salamis seemed too early after hoards, die sequences, and the results of scientific analysis were investigated. The idea that the decadrachm recalled the surrender of Thasos around 463 B.C. became another likely theory, but Starr asserts that the battle of Eurymedon River yielded more loot and had the sort of political implications that would warrant a commemorative coin. At Eurymedon, Cimon defeated a Persian naval force and captured their camp, claiming Athenian dominance over the Greek mainland, the isles, and the Mediterranean Sea. The events at Eurymedon River seem to merit a coin such as the Athenian decadrachm, dating the issue to somewhere between 467 and 463 B.C.

650 B.C.   450   250   50   50   250   450   650   850   1050   1250   1450 A.D.

Notable for its substantial size and bold, Archaic-style depiction of the goddess Athena, this decadrachm may have been struck to commemorate a specific historical event—but what?

NAXOS TETRADRACHM

GREECE · CIRCA 460 B.C.

Actual size approx. 25 mm

In the 1960s these coins brought $10,000, but by the late '70s a collector would pay over $100,000 for one of the best examples. Now an Extremely Fine specimen would bring $250,000.

Naxos, a Greek city on the isle of Sicily, experienced a series of reversals of fortune in the fifth century B.C. In an effort to control the Naxians, whom he suspected of wanting their independence, the tyrant Hieron of Syracuse deported the people from their city in 476 B.C. Hieron intended to build up the population of his city, Syracuse, so that it would never be challenged by any other city in the region. The Naxians were able to return home in approximately 461 B.C., after the fall of Hieron's regime. This tetradrachm may have been the first struck upon their arrival, and the citizens obviously employed a master cutter to prepare the dies for it.

What great master created this coin?

The chief deity of the city was Dionysus, the god of wine and male fertility. His bearded head, wearing an ivy wreath, graces the obverse. The head is executed in the severe style, which represents a transition between the Archaic and classical styles. The hair and beard retain something of the patterning found in Archaic art. The profile of Dionysus and the shape of the beard are also typical of Archaic art, but the eye is rendered in profile—a clearly classical technique. The entire image has a freer, more natural feel than the earlier style, in part because the artist has allowed the beard, hair, and wreath to violate the dotted border surrounding the head.

On the reverse, Silenus, the (usually drunk) faithful companion of Dionysus, squats on the ground and raises a wine cup. The name of the city surrounds him. This depiction brings us fully into early classical art. It is an intricate composition involving the superimposition of elements of Silenus's body, as well as perspective foreshortening. The engraving is precise and elegant. Not only are the muscles well developed, but one actually sees the bone structure of Silenus's ribs and collarbone beneath them.

What great master created this coin? We do not know his name, but we do know that he also designed the unique tetradrachm of Aetna (see No. 22, page 18) and is therefore known as the Aetna Master. It is clear that he stood at the forefront among artists of his day and that the closest parallels to his work are to be found in the work of the best contemporaneous Athenian vase painters.

There are 61 of these magnificent coins on record, mostly in high grade and from a single pair of dies. Unfortunately, the obverse die eventually developed an unpleasant chip under the nose of Dionysus. Nevertheless, this is one of the most sought-after coins of the early classical period.

650 B.C.   450   250   50   50   250   450   650   850   1050   1250   1450 A.D.

The work of an unknown master artist, the Naxos tetradrachm is one of the most highly desired of early classical coins.
The exceptional rendering of Dionysus shows Archaic style giving way to a more relaxed and lyrical classicism.

AEGINA SEA TURTLE STATER

GREECE · 530-485 B.C.

Actual size approx. 20 mm

In the 1960s average coins cost $200 to $300, but by the late 1980s Extremely Fine coins were bringing $5,000 and up. Recently a large group came to market, which dropped the Extremely Fine price to $2,000, but now they are back up to $5,000. Most of these coins come quite worn—only Fine or less, which sell for $200 to $400.

T he island of Aegina, situated in the Aegean Sea midway between Attica and the Peloponnese, derives its name from a consort of Zeus. In Greek mythology, Aegina was the daughter of the river god Asopus and the nymph Metope. Zeus took Aegina to an island called Oenone, close to Attica. It was here that Aegina gave birth to her son Aeacus, who would later become king of the island, thereafter known as Aegina.

The Aeginetans were traders because their rocky island was poorly suited to agriculture. They made their living transporting and selling goods and raw materials produced by others. Success created surplus assets in the form of material goods, which had a short shelf life. It was for this reason that Aeginetan wealth was transformed into silver coin.

The staters of Aegina are regarded as the Western world's first coinage, and were introduced soon after the advent of coinage further east. These staters were also the first international trade coinage, and they circulated widely in the Mediterranean from the late sixth century until the fourth century B.C. Many show evidence of this long circulation in the form of small banking countermarks, which seem to guarantee that the coins were composed of good silver.

On the obverse of the Aegina staters is a loggerhead turtle with a row of very small dots down the center of its shell. The turtle motif may have been a symbolic representation of the Aeginetan ships that roamed the sea, or the badge of an important family—or it may have been adopted simply because it was

easy to engrave and produce in massive quantities. The reverse depicted a formless square incuse. This was later followed by an incuse divided into eight sections, which then evolved into the windmill-like mill-sail pattern. This finally developed into a five-part incuse made up of three rectangles and two triangles. The sea turtle on the obverse changed over time into a variety not found in nature, with exaggerated dots down the center of its back and a large heavy rim on the front of its shell.

In 456 B.C. Athens conquered Aegina. Thereafter the island's staters were coined depicting a land tortoise rather than a sea turtle—Aegina having lost its sea power. The tension between Aegina and Athens led Pericles, the great Athenian politician, to refer to the island as the "leme" or eyesore of the coastal city Peiraeus. Many turtles of Aegina remained in circulation across the known world for as much as a century after Aegina ceased to issue them. While these coins are common, high-grade coins are scarce, and any of the first issue (Milbank 1, above) are really rare.

650 B.C. 450 250 50 50 250 450 650 850 1050 1250 1450 A.D.

CNOSSUS MINOTAUR STATER

GREECE · CIRCA 450 B.C.

Actual size approx. 24 mm

In 1959 a Very Fine coin brought SFr 1,600; by 1970 that same coin fetched SFr 5,400. In 1989 another brought SFr 16,000, and in 2007 one brought over $100,000. These coins usually come somewhat worn, in only about Fine condition.

This coin refers to the imagined legendary past of Cnossus, a Greek city-state located on the isle of Crete. Long before this coin was struck in about 450 B.C., Cnossus was the center of the Minoan culture, a pre-Greek civilization that existed from about 2600 B.C. until its mysterious destruction around 1400, possibly by earthquake, invaders, or both. The Minoans were a highly advanced, literate, and artistic people who traveled the eastern half of the Mediterranean and traded with the peoples of Egypt and the Syrian coast. After the collapse of their civilization, Crete descended into a long, illiterate dark age. By the time the Greeks arrived there several hundred years later, all that remained were vague, distorted memories of its once glorious past and some visible remnants of the destroyed culture. The palace at Cnossus had been vastly greater than anything built in the subsequent regressive period. Upon seeing its size and complexity, and the frescoes and reliefs of bulls that decorated its now roofless walls, the Greeks mistook the structure for a maze or labyrinth, and created the story of the Minotaur and the labyrinth.

According to their legend, Minos, the king of Crete, had a labyrinth at Cnossus where he kept the Minotaur, a flesh-eating monster with the head of a bull and the body of a man. Minos forced the people of his empire (which the Greeks conveniently determined to have included mainland Greece) to provide an annual quota of humans to be thrown into the labyrinth, where they wandered, lost, until they were hunted down and eaten by the Minotaur. Finally, Theseus, the hero of the story, defeated and

killed the monster and found his way out of the labyrinth, escaping Minos's wrath. Theseus, the legend continued, went on to become king of Athens and free the Greek mainland from the tyrannical rule of Minos.

Despite the new settlements, Crete remained an economic and cultural backwater in comparison to Athens and other mainland centers, so it is not surprising that when this coin was struck in about 450 B.C., it was executed in an archaic style that had already passed out of favor at more progressive mints. However, the charming and mysterious style suits the dark theme of the coin, whose obverse portrays the Minotaur in the Archaic kneeling position. Appropriately, the depiction is forceful and strong rather than delicate or elegant. The reverse shows an abstract design representing the labyrinth, the scene of the adventure. The labyrinth was frequently used on the coins of Cnossus, sometimes in the form seen here, at other times square or even round. Clearly, there was no set idea of how the mythical labyrinth looked. The geometric form depicted on this particular coin adds to its Archaic feel, evoking the ancient myths of the city.

The story remained no more than a myth until Sir Arthur J. Evans began excavating the city in 1903 and discovered the previously unknown Bronze Age city of the Minoans.

Only about 20 of these coins are recorded in all silver denominations.

ATHENS TETRADRACHM

GREECE · 440 B.C.

Actual size approx. 24 mm

Special conditions dramatically change the prices of these coins, as is discussed on page 7. Average nice Extremely Fine coins in the 1960s brought $120; in the '70s, $400; in the '90s, $1,500; and now $2,000.

In the fifth century B.C., after the Persian wars, Athens grew to be the dominant power in Greece. By 440 B.C., it was apparent that a great war was inevitable, with Sparta and her allies on one side and Athens and the Delian League on the other. When war finally broke out in 431, Athens began to extract more and more silver from its allies.

> The massive quantities of tetradrachms produced after 431 B.C. supplied the civilized world with coinage for more than a century.

Around 520 B.C., Athens first produced tetradrachms with Athena's head on the obverse and her totem bird, the owl, on the reverse. Also found on the reverse were the first three letters of the city's name and an olive sprig. Later a crescent moon was added, probably referring to the victory at Marathon in 490 B.C. Despite the fact that Athenian art at this time took on a more classical form, the Athenians continued to issue tetradrachms in the old Archaic style. As the Peloponnesian war dragged on, the style of the tetradrachms markedly declined. The visage of Athena began to appear far less noble, and the owl began to resemble a lopsided oval, the feathers around its head becoming increasingly ragged.

By 406 B.C., the city had almost run out of silver, and tetradrachms were struck over a copper core as an emergency measure to facilitate local commerce. These were called "money of necessity" and were immortalized in the play *Frogs* by Aristophanes:

Our silver coins, all of purest Athenian make,

All of perfect die and metal, all the fairest of the fair,

All of the unequaled workmanship, proved and valued everywhere

Both among our own Greeks and distant barbarians—

These we do not use, but the recent worthless base coins

Of vile character and basest metal, now we always use instead.

(Translation courtesy Dr. David MacDonald)

Athens lost the war in 403, but with the recovery of the economy in 393 B.C., the population was allowed to exchange copper tetradrachms for silver. These new tetradrachms were no longer archaized, implementing the "profile" eye instead of the "almond-shaped" eye. The massive quantities of tetradrachms produced after 431 B.C. supplied the civilized world with coinage for more than a century and spawned many imitative issues. The issue was so large that probably more than 100,000 still exist. In ancient times, the Athenian tetradrachm was extremely popular, and its popularity continues to this day.

650 B.C.　450　250　50　50　250　450　650　850　1050　1250　1450 A.D.

Possibly the best-known ancient coin, the Athens tetradrachm retained the same design for more than a century. It is as popular now as when it was minted.

Actual size approx. 23 mm

These coins, of which thousands exist, are very popular. In the 1960s they sold for $75, but now Extremely Fine coins bring $400 to $600, with Very Fine examples going for about $300. Coins with mythological reverses bring much more.

For much of Greek history, Thebes was the third most important Greek city-state, but during the fourth century B.C. it rose briefly to become the greatest power in Greece. The importance of Thebes is reflected in its issue of numerous silver staters.

The importance of Thebes is reflected in its issue of numerous silver staters.

The obverse of these coins features a shield of peculiar shape known as a *Boeotian* shield or, more correctly, a heroic shield. The shield, with its odd side openings, was associated in art with the heroes of Greek myth. Many Greek legends were connected to Thebes, and these stories continue to reverberate today. For instance, the myth of *Seven Against Thebes* inspired the Japanese director Akira Kurosawa's *Seven Samurai*, which Hollywood turned into *The Magnificent Seven*.

The reverse of this stater shows an amphora, sometimes decorated with ivy leaves. The amphora is emblematic of Dionysus, the god of wine, a major deity in Thebes. The reverse field contains the abbreviated name of a magistrate, and the names of many of the famous figures of Theban history appear on these coins.

Most notable is Epaminondas, the chief architect of Theban power, who was killed in battle in 362 B.C.

Some other reverses without the amphora have mythical themes, mainly depicting Heracles or Dionysus in various poses and stages of their lives. Here we show an example of a reverse depicting the infant Heracles killing the serpents that Hera sent to kill him.

Actual size approx. 24 mm

There are many reverse types for these coins, which vary greatly in value. In the late 1950s they sold for SFr 1,600 to 2,950; by the '70s, for SFr 7,500; in the '80s, for about the same; and now for about $15,000.

Melos, an island located about 100 miles east of the Peloponnesus, was colonized by the Phoenicians and later Hellenized by the Dorians. It was a quiet, sleepy little island for most of its history, but in the middle of the Peloponnesian War it suddenly became the object of Athenian imperialism. Because their ancestors had been settlers from the Peloponnesus, the Melians, feeling it would be sacrilegious to fight against their relatives, had allied themselves with Sparta against Athens. They attempted to remain neutral, but the Athenians would not allow it. The staters of Melos appear to have been coined to pay for the defense of the island state. Athens, angered at its neutrality, conquered Melos in 416 B.C. and summarily put all the men to death, sold the women and children into slavery, and melted all the coinage save a few small hoards.

On the obverse, most of the staters feature what was long thought to be a pomegranate but is now recognized as an apple.

The first coins known to come from Melos were found by some children in 1907. Of the 12 coins they found, eight were acquired by a Mr. R. Jameson, a noted Scottish collector living in Paris. By 1909 another 79 coins had been found, bringing the total to 91. In a 1964 article, the great numismatist Colin Kraay wrote that he could account for 84 of the coins in about 18 different types—although there has been some disagreement as to what constitutes a separate type and what may simply be a variation of a type. Additional specimens have appeared in more recently discovered hoards, but only a few specimens are known of each variety, making the staters of Melos almost legendary rarities among advanced collectors. All are executed in bold, attractive design and seem to date from the last third of the fifth century B.C.

On the obverse, most of the staters feature what was long thought to be a pomegranate but is now recognized as an apple. The reverses show a wide variety of types, including geometric designs, flowers, dolphins, a ram's head, gorgons, triskeles, and the head of a young warrior. The mystery of the reverse varieties is that they all seem to have been struck at the same time. One possibility is that the individuals responsible for the coins put their own types on the coins they produced.

ACRAGAS SKYLLA TETRADRACHM

GREECE · 420 B.C.

Actual size approx. 28 mm

In 1968 a tetradrachm fetched SFr 55,100; in 1976, SFr 126,000. Recently one brought $160,000 in New York, while a few years ago one broke $200,000. When exquisite expensive coins come to market the air is very thin and a very few collectors make the market on a given day depending on who already has the coin and who needs it.

Acragas, located on the southern shore of Sicily, was the second-largest Greek city on the island. It controlled rich agricultural land and was well situated for trade. However, the city's close proximity to territories controlled by Carthage ensured that it was always in the front lines during the frequent conflicts between the Greeks and Carthaginians. From approximately 500 B.C. to 430 B.C., the coins of Acragas were skillfully engraved but conservative in design, featuring a standing eagle on one side and a crab on the other. About 430 B.C., new coin engravers introduced a more developed classical design and future issues took on an innovative, adventurous style. Virtually all the coins struck in the quarter century after 430 B.C. are amazing works of art. The great Acragas decadrachm from this period is one of the most famous coins in the world, and its image is reproduced in many works about Greek art—but none of the other coins of Acragas exceed the Skylla tetradrachm.

The Skylla tetradrachm was struck about 420 B.C. On the obverse two magnificent eagles perch on a lifeless hare. One throws its head back in a scream of triumph as the other bends down as if to tear at its prey. Each feather is studied and delicately engraved. This strong composition is beautifully balanced and executed, skillfully filling the field of the coin. The initial letters of the city's name also appear in the field.

Although the obverse is brilliantly conceived and executed, the reverse is even more magnificent. The crab, traditional badge of Acragas, occupies the upper part of the design. It has been so skillfully depicted that it appears to be alive. Below the crab is a wonderful, mythic sea creature, the Skylla. She has the head and torso of a woman but beneath them the foreparts of two hounds and the tail of a sinuous sea monster. She is depicted in rapid action, cutting through the ocean, her hair streaming behind her, the sea-monster tail in quick convoluted motion, one human arm raised to shade her eyes as she scans the horizon. It is a magnificently baroque composition, skillfully filling the lower half circle of the coin die. The crab and the Skylla symbolize the importance of the sea to Acragas, and the skill and beauty of the composition attest to the city's sophistication and wealth.

Fewer than 20 of these wonderful coins are recorded.

Virtually all the Acragas coins struck in the quarter century after 430 B.C. are amazing works of art.

650 B.C.   450   250   50   50   250   450   650   850   1050   1250   1450 A.D.

ZEUS OLYMPIC STATER

GREECE · 416 B.C.

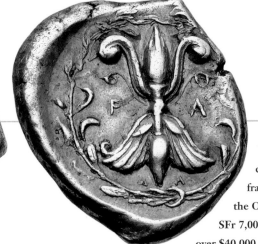

Actual size approx. 23 mm

With the exception of the coin illustrated here, this rare issue always comes very worn. In 1984, a example in Fine brought 8,500 French francs in Paris. This same coin was in the Leu numismatic auction of the Olympic coins of the BCD collection in 2004 in Zurich and sold for SFr 7,000. The coin illustrated, which is the finest known, sold in 2005 for over $40,000. Today it would probably bring $65,000.

The Greeks were devoted to athletics, and many cities had great athletic festivals, but in ancient Greece it was universally acknowledged that the greatest of all were the Olympic games. Traditionally believed to have been established in 776 B.C., the Olympic games were celebrated every four years at Olympia in the Peloponnesus, the site of ancient and impressive temples of Zeus, the king of the gods, and Hera, his wife and the goddess of married life. All of the contestants were men, and they competed in the nude. Only one woman was allowed to observe, a married woman who represented Hera. If any female virgin was caught watching the games, she was stoned.

This coin marks the first time Zeus makes an appearance on an Olympic coin.

People from every corner of Greece and from Greek colonies throughout the Mediterranean crowded into Olympia to see the games. Some common currency was needed, and from 510 B.C. until a little after 191 B.C., two mints, associated with the temples of Zeus and Hera, turned out coins for visitors to the festival. When visitors to the games turned in their own coins to be exchanged for the Olympic issues of the current games, there is no doubt that they were charged an exchange fee of some kind. According to Charles Seltman's 1921 book *Temple Coins of Olympia*, 364 different die combinations were used in this coinage, with only a few more having been discovered since then. New types were issued for the games held every four years, and they were so beautiful and meaningful that many seem to have been carried home as mementos.

The highlight of this long series, the head of Zeus wearing a wild-olive wreath, was created for the 91st Olympics in 416 B.C. The reverse of the coin has in the center a winged thunderbolt within a wild-olive wreath. The letters F and A are on either side of the thunderbolt. Below the thunderbolt are the two small letters "DA," probably the artist's signature. This coin marks the first time Zeus makes an appearance on an Olympic coin. It is believed that this Zeus head was directly inspired by the gold-and-ivory statue of Zeus by Phidias that stood in the temple of Zeus at Olympia. This Zeus head is different from later ones, which depict Zeus wearing a laurel wreath. According to Seltman, and as confirmed by our research, only seven of these coins are recorded. Most are in very worn condition, including the specimen in the British Museum in London, which probably has the best collection of ancient coins in the world.

Actual size approx. 35 mm

There are many varieties of Kimons, but the type discussed here is the most popular one. Major factors are condition, centering, and whether the coin was struck with a rusty die. A coin in the famous 1974 "Kunstfreundes" sale brought SFr 275,000, and nine years later in a weaker market it brought the same price. In 1987 two other specimens went for SFr 55,000 and 62,000. Today the 1974 coin would bring $250,000 or more, while others might only make $40,000 to $50,000.

The settlement that would eventually become the city of Syracuse was established by the Corinthians in the eighth century B.C. on the tiny island of Ortygia, off the coast of Sicily. The settlement grew wealthy and powerful so rapidly that within the next hundred years it expanded onto the larger island of Sicily and founded colonies of its own at Akrai, Kasmenai, and Camarina. Most of the silver tetradrachms and decadrachms of Syracuse display the head of the nymph Arethusa surrounded by dolphins, recalling Ortygia and the dolphins in the sea around it.

> Most of the silver tetradrachms and decadrachms of Syracuse display the head of the nymph Arethusa surrounded by dolphins.

The first decadrachms by the master engraver Kimon were issued about 415 B.C. and were struck from only three obverse dies and 12 reverse dies. The obverse shows a quadriga in full gallop with a flying Nike, the personification of victory, crowning its driver. Below the exergue line are a shield, a spear, a piece of body armor, a Phrygian helmet, and the Greek letters spelling ATHEL. The letters indicate that the weaponry, captured when the Athenians invaded Sicily, was meant to be awarded as prizes in athletic games.

The reverse, which is the more important side of the coin, shows the nymph Arethusa wearing an ampyx—an accessory used to hold long hair in a bun on the back of the head—and a pearl necklace. There are four dolphins surrounding her head; the name of the city is written above the back of her head. While some of the 12 reverse dies are unsigned, others are signed two or three times. On the coin pictured here, the signature of the artist, KIMON, appears on the dolphin just below Arethusa's neck. The earliest variety of this decadrachm also shows a dolphin swimming out from under her neck.

Impressive by virtue of its size as well as its artistry, the decadrachm of Syracuse by master artist Kimon employs the visual iconography of victory in its design.

EUAINETOS DECADRACHM

GREECE · 412-393 B.C.

Actual size approx. 36 mm

In 1957 a signed decadrachm brought SFr 7,100, but in 1976 the same coin sold by the same company fetched SFr 50,000. As with the coins of Kimon, the quality, centering, and (to a lesser degree) presence or absence of signature greatly affect the price. The best can cost $200,000, while most are traded at $15,000 to $30,000.

Euainetos was an engraver at the Syracuse mint and a contemporary of the engraver Kimon. Euainetos, however, was significantly more prolific. While Kimon produced only 3 decadrachm obverse dies, Euainetos created 24. Although many of his dies are unsigned, they are clearly recognizable as his work. His compositions are characterized by their simplicity and realism, and by a fine sense of proportion. Euainetos was at the forefront of the modern art movement of his time, the high classical style, with its dynamic tension between idealism and realism. His flexibility as an artist and his willingness to learn from his colleague are apparent in his style, which grew and evolved over time. Euainetos's dies are as refined as Kimon's, but are bolder and more self-assured. This boldness is evident in the artist's signature at the bottom of the die, which is as big as the name of the city over Arethusa's head. In spite of having been influenced by Kimon's work, Euainetos's designs have been reproduced far more often, and are still being reproduced today. In fact, the Euainetos decadrachm is the most copied coin of all time.

On the obverse is a racing quadriga, over which flies Nike, shown crowning the chariot driver. Below the exergual ground line is a shield, a crested helmet, and a cuirass between two greaves. Here we see Euainetos's style fully developed. The figures are boldly and deeply cut. The swirling drapery of Nike and the charioteer reflects contemporary Athenian sculpture. The juxtaposition and superimposition of the horses' legs impart a distinct feeling of movement. The wheels of the chariot demonstrate a well-studied understanding of perspective.

> The work is bold and precise—the signs of a master who knew exactly what he was doing and why.

On the reverse, which is often mistaken for the obverse because of its subject, is an apple-cheeked head of the water nymph Arethusa wearing a reed wreath in her hair, a pearl necklace, and a triple-pendant earring. The artwork reveals Kimon's influence in the sweetness of Arethusa's face, but Euainetos's version is stronger and more mature. The head is surrounded by four dolphins, representing the sea. Above and to the left of the head is the name of the city, and below it is the name of the artist. In various places near her head, some varieties include an additional symbol, such as a griffin head or a cockleshell. Overall, the work is bold and precise—the signs of a master who knew exactly what he was doing and why. Because the signature of the artist is at the bottom of the reverse it is rarely complete, as parts are usually off the flan.

650 B.C.   450   250   50 | 50   250   450   650   850   1050   1250   1450 A.D.

The most copied coin in history, the Euainetos decadrachm displays the influence of the Kimon decadrachm but surpasses
it in maturity and strength.

Actual size approx. 25 mm

In 1934 a Very Fine coin cost SFr 2,500 at auction; in 1958, SFr 18,250; in 1974 the price was SFr 90,000, and in 2004 at Numismatica Ars Classica the price was SFr 138,000. In 2000 a great example topped SFr 300,000. A very average coin of the second die might bring $25,000, while the best example of the first die could surpass $400,000.

The obverse of this coin features the facing head of the water nymph Arethusa, wearing an earring, a necklace, and an ampyx, a ribbon restraining her hair. Four dolphins playfully surround her, and above and outside the circle the name ARETHUSA is engraved.

One cannot help but wonder if the artist Kimon was in love with a beautiful girl when he created this incredible die, for the image of Arethusa is perfect in every way. This coin is, simply, a masterpiece. The beauty of Arethusa and her soulful gaze cannot be denied. Her flowing hair is rendered in delicate, exquisite detail. The engraver Kimon has proudly signed his name on the ampyx, directly over her forehead.

The reverse is equally well done. The charioteer struggles with the reins to control his unruly horses, which turn their heads, each differently, giving a feeling of power and motion. Above the racing figures, Nike flies to crown the victorious team. The wings and garments of Nike and the garments of the quadriga driver swivel with movement, and the well-articulated musculature of the horses again impresses the viewer with its power. In the exergue

there is an ear of barley and the name of the city. Kimon signed the reverse die also, this time on the exergue line.

> One cannot help but wonder if Kimon was in love with a beautiful girl when he created this incredible die.

Kimon's pride in the two dies he created for this issue is evident and surely justified, but the die we illustrate is vastly superior to a second die known to collectors. In the history of coinage few works have equaled and none exceeded Kimon's achievement here.

This coin competes with the Euainetos decadrachm for being the most copied coin in history, not only today but in ancient times as well.

650 B.C.   450   250   50   50   250   450   650   850   1050   1250   1450 A.D.

Was this the face that launched a thousand fakes? With its exquisite depiction of the nymph Arethusa, this coin is not only one of the most admired in history, but also one of the most copied.

CAMARINA DIDRACHM

GREECE · 410 B.C.

Actual size approx. 19 mm

This issue has always been important and sought after by collectors, but it usually comes in corroded condition; thus, the prices have been in the area of SFr 3,800 to 6,800. About 10 years ago the finest example sold for $50,000. In 2007 it came to auction and sold for over $100,000.

Camarina was colonized by Syracuse in 598 B.C. as part of Syracusan expansion in Sicily. It was located on a fertile plain between the Hipparis and Oanis rivers, and since the city had no seaport, the mouth of the Hipparis was widened and deepened to accommodate shipping. By the mid-sixth century B.C. Camarina had become quite influential, so much so that in 553 the city revolted against Syracuse. During the ensuing struggle, the Syracusans defeated the army of Camarina and expelled all of the city's inhabitants. In 552 B.C., new settlers were brought to the city for repopulation, and again it began to thrive. When war broke out in 491, Syracuse lost Camarina to neighboring Gela. By 485, however, it was back under Syracusan control, again depopulated. In 461 it was reinhabited, with many of the settlers coming from Gela. In 258 Camarina changed hands between Rome and Carthage during the First Punic War and was, to a large degree, destroyed.

The obverse of this didrachm shows a pattern of waves surrounding the facing head of the young river god Hipparis. He wears horns on his forehead, and locks of hair cascade on either side of his head like running water. The composition is completed by two freshwater mullets, residents of the city's lake. The signature of the artist, Euai[netos], appears inconspicuously on the young god's neck.

The reverse depicts the nymph Camarina, after whom the city was named. She is seated on the back of a swimming swan, her veil inflated by the wind, while a fish plays in the water.

During this period classical art grew ever more complex in the scenes it portrayed and increasingly emotional in its renditions of subjects.

This is a work of the late fifth century, about 410 B.C. During this period classical art grew ever more complex in the scenes it portrayed and increasingly emotional in its renditions of subjects. These trends, evident in the Athenian red figured pottery of the time, are also fully apparent in this coin. On the obverse, the river god meets the observer with a soulful, slightly wistful gaze. The scene on the reverse is simultaneously complex and graceful. The floating body of the swan is balanced by the billowing veil held by the nymph. The scene fills the round body of the coin admirably.

Fewer than 13 of these wonderful coins are recorded and, with the exception of one coin, they are all from the same pair of dies.

650 B.C.   450   250   50   50   250   450   650   850   1050   1250   1450 A.D.

GELA TETRADRACHM

Actual size approx. 25 mm

This issue always comes worn, ranging from about Fine to Very Fine. In 1959 one sold for SFr 8,500, and in 1977 the same coin sold by the same seller brought SFr 29,000. Today the price would be between $15,000 and $20,000.

Gela, located in southern Sicily, was one of the wealthiest Greek colonies on the island. It sits on the coast by the mouth of the river Gelas, which gave the city its name. The river was regarded, as all ancient rivers were, as a local god, and most of the city's coinage bears the image of the river god conceived as a bull with the head of a man, reflecting both the animal strength of the rushing water and its more benevolent divine qualities. Occasionally, the river is personified in another manner, as on this important coin, a silver tetradrachm struck about 410 B.C.

Here we are in the presence of classical Greek art at its finest, combining idealism and realism, striving for innovation yet retaining a sense of order and balance.

On the obverse, Nike, goddess of victory, drives a slow quadriga. A laurel wreath, the symbol of victory, is seen in the field above, and the name of the city is visible in the exergue. Similar obverses were struck at other Sicilian cities, notably Leontini and Syracuse, celebrating the victories of local citizens in the aristocratic sport of chariot racing. On the Gela coins, however, Nike, the quadriga, and the horses are in perfect proportion, and each element is precisely rendered, creating a sense of quiet order and harmony.

Even more significant, the reverse shows the head of the river god Gelas, this time portrayed not as a man-headed bull but as a beautiful youth. The locks of his hair recall the ripples of water; he wears a taenia (narrow ribbon) in his hair and a small horn, a mark of divinity, on his forehead. He is surrounded by three mullets, fish native to his waters. The fish are not represented in simple profile, as a lesser artist might have done, but appear to move and twist. In an unparalleled innovation, the mullet behind Gelas's head is turned so that we glimpse its underside, while the one before his face is seen from below. Here we are in the presence of classical Greek art at its finest, combining idealism and realism, striving for innovation yet retaining a sense of order and balance.

Only about 20 specimens of this coin are recorded. In addition to being beautiful, it is clear that they circulated actively as money since most of the recorded examples are quite worn.

650 B.C.   450   250   50   50   250   450   650   850   1050   1250   1450 A.D.

41

ACRAGAS DECADRACHM

GREECE · 406 B.C.

Actual size approx. 35 mm

This coin has very few appearances because of its rarity. In 1977 a damaged coin brought SFr 140,000, but in 1996 the same coin fetched a mere SFr 55,000. The Hunt brothers' decadrachm held by Sotheby's in the early 1990s brought $572,000 on June 19, 1990, where it was the cover coin on the auction catalog. Today that coin would top the million-dollar mark.

Acragas, one of the grandest Greek cities in Sicily, was a wealthy center of advanced art and architecture. Located on the southern coast and relatively removed from other Greek cities, it was close to the territory of Carthage, a frequent enemy. Acragas also produced some of the most spectacular coins in history. This exceptional decadrachm appears to commemorate the victory of Exainetos, a prominent citizen of Acragas, at the Olympic Games. It is recorded that when he returned to the city, Exainetos was escorted by a procession of 300 chariots drawn by pairs of white horses.

> The beauty of these coins clearly indicates that Acragas employed some of the finest die cutters of the period.

The coin's obverse shows a speeding quadriga handled by a young driver whose single drapery billows in the wind. The quadriga is depicted at a slight angle toward the viewer. The horses are posed individually, their legs and hooves creating the dynamic illusion of movement. Above them we find the city's name and an eagle clutching a snake in its claws. A crab appears below the quadriga. The eagle is thought to represent the sun in its course through the sky, while the crab seems to signify the sea below.

The reverse shows two eagles, one with lowered head and the other with head raised, both perched on a hare on a rocky outcrop. The eagles are so realistically rendered that one can almost imagine the exuberant cry of the bird with its head thrown back. Behind the eagles is a grasshopper, presumably the personal badge of the official in charge of the coinage. The beauty of these coins clearly indicates that Acragas employed some of the finest die cutters of the period. Although neither side of this coin is signed (like some tetradrachms in the same series), it is thought that the famed engraver Myron executed the quadriga while his contemporary Polycrates created the eagles. Less than 10 of these magnificent coins are recorded today.

This decadrachm, along with the tetradrachms of the same series (see page 32), was issued during the last years of the city's existence, shortly before it was destroyed by the Carthaginians in 406 B.C.

650 B.C.   450   250   50   50   250   450   650   850   1050   1250   1450 A.D.

Some of the most spectacular coins in history were produced in the ancient city of Acragas. The decadrachm, a marvel of artistry, is exceedingly rare.

LARISSA DRACHM

GREECE · CIRCA 400–344 B.C.

Actual size approx. 20 mm

The early drachms of Larissa are all experimental and thus vary greatly in artistic quality and therefore in price. The illustrated coin is worth about $5,000, but lesser coins would have correspondingly lower prices. In the years before Catherine Lorber published her work on these coins they were thought to be later issues and were not recognized as being signed.

Larissa was the chief city of Thessaly, an area of central Greece named for Thessalos, son of the Greek demigod Heracles. The city, which took its name from the nymph Larissa, around whose spring it had grown up, was renowned for its agricultural abundance and its horses, which were reputed to be the finest in Greece. Not surprisingly, Larissa was also famous for its cavalry.

> During the early decades of this coinage, die cutters must have struggled with how best to depict the facing head of the nymph.

Beginning early in the fourth century B.C. and continuing until 344 B.C. (when Philip II of Macedonia conquered all of Thessaly), Larissa struck a series of silver drachms—and later didrachms—featuring a facing head of Larissa on the obverse and a horse on the reverse. During the early decades of this coinage, die cutters must have struggled with how best to depict the facing head of the nymph, because the first die cutter, who signed much of his work ΣIMO, produced portraits that vary widely in their attractiveness. The best of them are fresh and have a charming simplicity and the reverses display well-executed grazing horses.

In 1992, Catherine C. Lorber published 93 dies of this early, innovative series. The best of these is die 20, which shows a high-relief portrait of the nymph facing slightly left, with her left shoulder raised to indicate she is throwing a ball. (The legend is that while chasing the ball she had thrown, Larissa fell into the stream that came to bear her name, and drowned.) The signature, AI, of the city's best artist appears above Larissa's head. On the reverse is a grazing horse. This single die is a remarkable work of Greek art; only about five are recorded.

The later drachms of Larissa are more stereotypical, but still undeniably attractive. The head of this Larissa is modeled after Kimon's facing head of Arethusa on the coins of Syracuse, but the dies were mass produced and lack the delicacy and originality of the works of Kimon, or of the engraver AI who signed the earlier Larissa dies.

SYRACUSE ARETHUSA
100-LITRA COIN

GREECE · 390–380 B.C.

Actual size approx. 15 mm

These were frequently struck with rusty and broken dies, which makes well-struck coins from fresh dies much more valuable. In the 1960s SFr 7,000 was the price; in 1975 they brought $7,250, and in one exceptional moment in 1988 an example brought $40,000. The normal price today is $16,500 for a nice example.

The obverse of this small gold coin shows the head of the water nymph Arethusa wearing a necklace, an elaborate earring, and a hairnet (splendone) embroidered with a star pattern. The name of the city is before her face and the signature of the artist, EUAI[NETOS] or KI[MON], is behind her head.

> The artist has here arranged the combat between Heracles and the lion to conform to the circular flan of the coin, giving the coin and the design a feeling of organic wholeness.

On the reverse, Heracles kneels on uneven ground and wrestles the Nemean lion, representing the first of his 12 mythological labors.

The face of Arethusa is exceptionally sweet. She is shown here as a young goddess. Her hair is elaborately arranged and carefully engraved, as are the hairnet and jewelry, all without robbing the face of its fresh innocence.

The reverse is even more impressive. The artist has here arranged the combat between Heracles and the lion to conform to the circular flan of the coin, giving the coin and the design a feeling of organic wholeness. The musculature of both Heracles and the lion is beautifully defined and creates a feeling of balance and dynamic symmetry.

These 100-litra coins were also known as gold double decadrachms and were either unsigned or signed by Euainetos or Kimon. One problem that these coins frequently have is that many were struck with badly rusted dies, which would indicate that the dies were highly valued and reused over many years and stored in the interim.

This coin is a little gem, an example of great art in a small space. As many as 2,000 of these coins may still exist.

650 B.C.　450　250　50　50　250　450　650　850　1050　1250　1450 A.D.

CARTHAGINIAN DIDO TETRADRACHM

GREECE · 380–300 B.C.

Actual size approx. 25 mm

These pieces are always wanted by collectors. One specimen brought SFr 18,000 in 1970, but by 1976 the price at auction was $56,000. These coins do not come up very often, and the specimens are always in good Very Fine condition. The current value is about $50,000.

Carthage, the great commercial city-state on the coast of north Africa, never used coinage until it colonized parts of Sicily where the inhabitants used coinage in their everyday business. The entire Siculo-Punic coinage period ran from 380 to 300 B.C. Among these coins, the most spectacular and innovative are those bearing the head of Dido. Dido was a legendary princess of Tyre who fled her homeland when her brother Pygmalion became king and murdered her husband. She went on to found Carthage in 814 B.C.

> The dies by the Punic artists have sharper, harder features, while the Greek artists produced finer dies with softer, sweeter, more refined features.

There are three different types of Dido obverses. Two show her wearing a Phrygian cap, but the third has what appears to be a pleated linen tiara resembling a seashell. On the reverse of all three versions is a walking lion with his head turned toward the viewer, and a palm tree in the background. The lion walks on an exergue line below which in Punic is written "People of the Camp," indicating this was a military issue. Of the Phrygian-cap types, 16 coins were known to Kenneth Jenkins, as well as 15 of the seashell-tiara type. Jenkins published all of the known Siculo-Punic dies in the *Swiss Numismatic Review* from 1971 to 1978.

The dies for the entire series were executed by both Greek and Punic artists. The dies by the Punic artists have sharper, harder features, while the Greek artists produced finer dies with softer, sweeter, more refined features. The rest of the coinage featured a head of either Arethusa or Tanit, or a Heracles head of the Alexander type on the obverse. The reverse type is a horse's head with a palm tree or, less commonly, a full horse and palm tree.

650 B.C.   450   250   50   50   250   450   650   850   1050   1250   1450 A.D.

CLAZOMENAE TETRADRACHM

GREECE · CIRCA 375 B.C.

Actual size approx. 26 mm

This signed coin has never come up for sale in this or the last century, but if it did it would bring over $500,000. In the 1970s there emerged a group of specimens that were of poor artistic quality and in a corroded state of preservation. The coins from that group bring about $3,500, but they bear no relationship to the coin shown here.

The city of Clazomenae is on today's mainland Turkey and on a nearby island in the Gulf of Smyrna. The first badge of the city was a winged boar, large numbers of which, according to legend, had once infested the area. Clazomenae is one of the cities that struck early coins of electrum. After 387 B.C. they struck the Apollo and swan tetradrachms for which the city is most numismatically famous. The swan is associated with Apollo and is said to have flourished in the delta of the Hermus. The name of the city could have been derived from the sounds that swans make.

Despite the tremendous production, the tetradrachms are excessively rare today—so rare that this coin has never appeared in any auction.

On the obverse of the coin is an exceptionally fine head of Apollo facing slightly left. The relief is high and the flowing locks of hair that frame his face are executed with great delicacy. The face itself is beautiful and strong, with expressive eyes and well-marked brow and cheekbones. It is a face that expresses both power and grace. The artist who created this coin must have been proud of his work. He has placed the unusually complete and explicit artist signature "Theodotus Made It" in the left field.

A realistic and graceful swan flutters its wings on the reverse. Again, the relief is high and the image majestic, with economy of lines. Surrounding the swan are the initial letters of the city's name and the name of the magistrate responsible for the issue.

Theodotus of Clazomenae cut many dies for the city, all works of art, over a period of at least 20 years. Despite the tremendous production, the tetradrachms are excessively rare today—so rare that this coin has never appeared in any auction, and only about three are recorded, all of them in museums. Theodotus also created a wonderful gold stater of rarity equal to the aforementioned tetradrachm. A group of unsigned tetradrachms appeared on the market in the 1970s; while imaginative, they were not struck from dies cut by the master.

650 B.C.   450   250   50   50   250   450   650   850   1050   1250   1450 A.D.

RHODES TETRADRACHM

Actual size approx. 24 mm

Early Rhodian tetradrachms have come up for sale in 1977, when one brought SFr 10,500, and in 1986, when one in the Leu sale reached SFr 40,000. More recently the prices have been widely varied, but the best bring from $35,000 to $70,000. Coins that are not of exquisite style can cost $10,000 in Extremely Fine, and later ones with the sun rays behind Helios's head command $2,500 to $7,500 in Extremely Fine.

The isle of Rhodes, off the southern coast of Anatolia, was originally the home of three separate Greek colonies. In 408 B.C., the three combined to found a new capital, which bore the same name as the island, Rhodes. The new city required a new god. Helios, the sun god often equated with Apollo, was the chief deity of the island and regularly appeared on the obverse of Rhodes's coins.

The earliest facing heads of Helios, such as those on the specimens illustrated here, may have been inspired by Kimon's facing head of Arethusa on the coins of Syracuse. If so, the die cutter adapted his inspiration appropriately to his subject. According to Charles Seltman, the artist who created these dies had such a powerful imagination and painterly technique that he must have been a painter. The hair of Helios fans out in obvious imitation of the rays of the sun, and the sun god gazes directly at the observer with no hint of the slight shyness of Arethusa. The result is a thoroughly wonderful portrait of the young Helios in his midday strength, struck in very high relief.

The reverse bears a rose, the flower for which the island was named and for which it remains famous today. The flower is well studied from nature but also has a nice sense of pattern about it. The reverse retains its shallow incuse, a remnant of the simple square punches that occupied the reverse of the earliest Greek coins. The examples illustrated, which are struck from the same pair of dies, bear the artist's signature "ΞΕΝΟ," which is

virtually unknown on coins of Rhodes as well as nearly all the coins of Asia Minor.

On later coins of Rhodes, the face of Helios became rounder and fleshier, and the artists introduced actual sun rays, rather than utilizing the god's hair to suggest them. Workmanship, while still attractive, became stereotyped and lacked originality.

Oddly, during the Middle Ages the head of Helios on the coins of Rhodes was mistaken for the portrait of Christ in glory, and the rose on the reverse was taken for the biblical Rose of Sharon. These coins were believed to have been the 30 pieces of silver paid to Judas, miraculously transformed to bear Christ's portrait.

650 B.C.   450   250   50   50   250   450   650   850   1050   1250   1450 A.D.

AMPHIPOLIS TETRADRACHM

Actual size approx. 25 mm

The quality of the art in these coins varies tremendously, so we will consider only the better dies. In 1959 the price for one of these was SFr 14,400, but by 1975 the price was SFr 60,000, and in 1990 an example brought SFr 150,000. Today the value of a great coin is probably $150,000.

Amphipolis was located on a hill in northeastern Greece three miles from the Aegean Sea. The river Strymon encircled the city on three sides, making it the most defensible site in the area. The first recorded name for the city was *Anadraimos*, which in Greek means "nine roads." The Greeks most likely selected the name because Anadraimos was crisscrossed by trade routes linking the kingdoms of Thrace and Macedonia. Some of the trade items that passed through Anadraimos were ship timber, pitch, tar, silver, and gold. The combination of natural resources and location was remarkable, and the town became very important to the Greeks.

> This head of Apollo is among the most impressive ones depicted on all Greek coinage.

In the early fifth century B.C., two Thracian tribes, the Bisaltai and the Edoni, populated the area. In 479 B.C. this is where Alexander I of Macedonia destroyed the last vestiges of Persia's troops after the battle of Plataea. The Athenians absorbed Anadraimos in 437, renaming it Amphipolis. The city achieved independence following the end of the Peloponnesian War in 403, but fell to Philip of Macedonia in 357 B.C.

Between about 369 and 353 B.C., Amphipolis produced some of the most magnificent Greek coins of the period. The obverse of this tetradrachm portrays a three-quarter facing head of Apollo, wearing a laurel wreath. Apollo's splendid image combines idealism with naturalism, both hallmarks of the classical style. The massive curls that frame Apollo's handsome face almost swallow the delicate laurel wreath. The facial planes are subtly modeled, the eyes direct and clear. This head of Apollo is among the most impressive ones depicted on all Greek coinage.

The reverse shows a lighted race-torch surrounded by a broad, square border bearing the city's name. A small laurel wreath, symbol of victory, accompanies the torch within its border. Fifty different obverse dies were created for tetradrachms during this period, and some of the earlier dies are considered artistic failures. The dies created after Philip II took the city are considered to be the very best.

650 B.C.   450   250   50   50   250   450   650   850   1050   1250   1450 A.D.

PHILIP II TETRADRACHM

GREECE · 359-336 B.C.

Actual size approx. 25 mm

When looking at these coins we must view them as two separate classes. The high-style lifetime ones have always brought $3,000 to $8,500, and prices have not changed much because the collecting public confuses them with the far more common and stylistically poor posthumous issues, which sell for $1,000 to $2,000 in Mint State.

Before Philip II came to the throne of Macedonia, the kingdom was weak, poorly organized, and insignificant both militarily and economically. In the course of his brilliant career, Philip first became sovereign of Macedonia, and soon took control of all of Greece. Even so, he was not immune to prejudice. He may have been the king of Macedonia, but Macedonians were not Greek. They spoke a different language and were less cultured than the Greeks, who considered them to be ruffians. In the words of one Athenian aristocrat, they drank their wine straight, without mixing it with water. Philip and his son Alexander were extremely important and very powerful and the Greeks feared them, but they did not respect them. Nevertheless, Philip contended that he was a true Greek, a descendant of the ancient Homeric hero Achilles. He backed up his claim with a victory in the Olympic Games, for only true Greeks were permitted to participate at Olympia. This coin, then, attests to Philip's status as a Greek among Greeks, not merely some northern barbarian. His acceptance as a Greek also aided in Philip's unification of the Greek city-states, without which Alexander the Great could not have gone on to conquer most of the known world.

The primary silver coins of Philip II are tetradrachms bearing an anepigraphic (without legends) portrait of Zeus on the obverse, and a massive muscular horse ridden by a slim, youthful jockey on the reverse. The horse, one of Philip's own racehorses, had won the race in the Olympic Games that had proved the ruler's Greek pedigree. Later issues, struck under his sons, became greatly degraded artistically. The portrait of Philip lost its nobility; the horse grew smaller and more doglike, while the jockey grew progressively larger.

This coin attests to Philip's status: he was not merely some northern barbarian.

What is thought to be the tomb of Philip II was discovered in 1977 in Vergina, Greece. It contained among its treasures two small ivory heads—one of Philip II and one of Alexander. The head of Philip II is virtually identical to the head of Zeus on Philip's coins, indicating that the image actually depicts Philip himself portrayed in the guise of Zeus. The significance of this determination is that it marks Philip II as the first Greek of the Hellenistic era to put his own portrait on a coin. The tomb also contained Philip II's bones and personal armor.

Philip's silver tetradrachms were so widely accepted that they were also minted by his son, Alexander the Great; by the weak-minded Philip III; and by several kings who followed them. In addition, they were so widely dispersed that they were copied by the German Celtic tribes as the primary pattern for their coinage, as well as by tribes in Gaul, Britain, and Eastern Europe.

650 B.C.   450   250   50   50   250   450   650   850   1050   1250   1450 A.D.

Actual size approx. 21 mm

There are thousands of coins of Metapontum struck from 200-plus dies, but the three-quarters-facing-head type described here is a true marvel. The price record is impressive as well: in the much-cited 1974 sale held in Zurich by Bank Leu and Münzen und Medaillen, this coin fetched SFr 145,000, and in Sotheby's 1990 Hunt sale the same coin opened at $13,000 but reached $185,000, which struck some as cheap at the time. Today that coin might reach $300,000 or more.

Metapontum was a Greek colony in southern Italy, located on an extremely fertile plain between two rivers. In fact, the name *Metapontum* means "between the rivers." It is not surprising that the coinage of Metapontum regularly featured an ear of grain: the city's wealth came largely from its bountiful grain crops that were exported throughout the Mediterranean.

> This innovative pose required the creation of new techniques in perspective and foreshortening, resulting in a remarkably individualized, asymmetrical portrait.

The earliest coinage, from the sixth and early fifth centuries B.C., had grain ears on both the obverse and the reverse, one side raised in relief and the other sunk in incuse. In later periods, the grain ear was restricted to the reverse. For about a century, beginning around 400 B.C., the city issued a long series of silver staters called *nomoi* (singular: nomos) depicting the heads of various deities and heroes on the obverse, and the ear of grain on the reverse. Virtually all of these staters are competently executed, and many are splendid works of art. One in particular, struck about 340 B.C., is a masterpiece.

The obverse of this coin shows the head of the god Dionysus wearing an ivy wreath. Greek artists had mastered both profile and facing or near-facing heads well before this coin was struck, but here the artist portrays the god's face turned only slightly toward the viewer. This innovative pose required the creation of new techniques in perspective and foreshortening, resulting in a remarkably individualized, asymmetrical portrait. The god is shown as a confident youth with almost feminine features, including a thin nose, cupped bow lips, and piercing eyes. In contrast, the hair is a mass of heavy curls that almost swallows the ivy wreath worn upon it. Behind the head are the Greek letters KAL, which may be the initials of the artist who created the die, a mint official, a government official, or possibly only one individual who may have held two or even all three of these positions.

The reverse bears a barley ear, which was the standard reverse type on the silver stater during this period. On a leaf of the barley stalk is a coiled snake and below it is the name "Philo" in Greek, both referring to officials in charge of the coinage. Only three specimens of this fantastic coin are recorded, and the illustrated example is by far the finest known.

PANTICAPAEUM
GOLD STATER

GREECE · CIRCA 340 B.C.

Actual size approx. 20 mm

In the early 1990s these coins were difficult to sell at $21,000. More recently they reached $70,000, but now they have settled at $35,000 to $40,000. The three-quarters-facing-head type brings about $175,000. None of these coins seem to have seen circulation, as they are never in condition worse than Extremely Fine.

Panticapaeum was a Greek colony founded in the seventh century B.C. by the Milesians and located in what is now the city of Kerch on the eastern shore of Crimea. The ancient city, a capital of the kingdom of the Cimmerian Bosporus, was ruled by kings who respected and made use of the institutions of cities within their kingdom. When the kingdom grew rich in the fourth century B.C., chiefly through the export of grain to Greece and Anatolia, that wealth was largely converted into a series of splendid gold staters, of which this issue is the most outstanding.

The obverse of the stater shows the head of a satyr either in profile or in a three-quarter frontal pose, while the reverse depicts a griffin grasping a broken spear in its mouth and standing on an ear of grain. The head on the obverse is beautifully executed, with the face fully modeled and the hair skillfully rendered, imposing an overall sense of design on the wildness of the creature. Because satyrs were generally associated with northern lands and because King Satyrus I had been largely responsible for the growth and prosperity of the kingdom, his successors used the satyr type in his memory. The image is often mistaken for that of the Greek god Pan, possibly because of the spelling of the city's name. The name *Panticapaeum*, however, has nothing to do with Pan; it derives from the fact that the city was a center of fishing and trade and can be translated as "fish road." A further indication that this is not the head of Pan is that it exhibits the ass's ears and button nose of a satyr, rather than Pan's horns and goat's face.

The griffin on the reverse is another mythological creature that was associated with northern lands, but it was also associated with gold. In this instance the griffin stands on the real source of Panticapaeum's gold—not mines, but crops of golden grain. The initial letters of the city's name appear in the field.

Because King Satyrus I had been largely responsible for the growth and prosperity of the kingdom, his successors used the satyr type in his memory.

Reflecting the wealth of the area, these gold staters originally carried a weight of 9.42 grams, giving each the same value as a Cyzicus electrum stater. However, when the Philip II gold staters became the dominant coinage, the Panticapaeum coin was reduced in weight to 9.07 grams.

650 B.C.   450   250   50 | 50   250   450   650   850   1050   1250   1450 A.D.

TARENTUM HORSEMAN STATER

GREECE · 340–325 B.C.

Actual size approx. 22 mm

There are more than 100 different types and variants of Tarentum staters, yet one very wonderful die is our focus here. In 1986 a nice but slightly off-center example brought 680 deutsche marks in Munich. This coin has such a complex design that it is very difficult to get it all on the flan, yet it all needs to be there for the full impact of the artistry to be realized. A centered Extremely Fine coin should be worth $7,500. Most nice Tarentum coins cost from $400 to $1,500 if reasonably well centered.

The Greeks colonized Sicily and southern Italy, founding there a number of independent city-states. One of the earliest foundations was Taras, more commonly called Tarentum, the Latin form of the name.

These variations on the theme have produced one of the most charming series of Greek coins.

Legend tells that there was a native Italian town on the site long before the Greeks came to Italy and that the native settlement had been founded by Taras, a son of the god Poseidon, under unusual circumstances. Taras was cast into the sea by a shipwreck and only survived because Poseidon sent a dolphin to carry him to shore—and on the spot where he landed he founded the town. Later, about 708 B.C. according to tradition, Greeks came to the site. The legend claims the colonists were from Sparta but were sent away because they were of illegitimate birth, the product of relations between Spartan women and helots (unfree agricultural serfs) during a time when the Spartan men were away at a long war.

Tarentum prospered greatly, becoming the largest and richest of the Greek cities in Italy. The city first struck coins about 510 B.C., and from the beginning the coinage featured the figure of Taras riding on a dolphin. About 415 B.C., Tarentum began to strike its most famous series of coins, the silver staters known as "horsemen." On one side, Taras always rides a dolphin, occasionally accompanied by stylized waves. On the other is a horseman. Each issue was a new composition, presenting the horseman in new form. Sometimes he is a mature man in armor, armed with a lance and occasionally leading a second horse. On other issues the horseman is a young naked rider, a race jockey, who may crown his horse with a victor's laurels or leap from the horse at the end of the race. Occasionally, he is accompanied by a second figure, restraining the horse or assisting the horseman in some other way.

These variations on the theme have produced one of the most charming series of Greek coins. The workmanship is consistently good, and sometimes the composition and die cutting combine to produce a genuine masterpiece.

The most innovative coin in the series was struck in the period from 340 to 325 B.C. The central figure is a prancing horse upon which sits a naked boy who is crowned by a flying Nike; the horse is embraced by another boy, who is nearly as tall as the animal. On the reverse, Taras is seated sideways on the dolphin with his head facing and turned slightly back as he prepares to spear a fish with his trident. To the left is a raised tablet upon which is the artist's faint signature, AP. The name of the city is to the right, and all is bordered by stylized waves. This coin is scarce, and well-struck examples are nearly impossible to find because of the complexity of the design.

650 B.C.   450   250   50   50   250   450   650   850   1050   1250   1450 A.D.

TARENTUM GOLD STATER

GREECE · 340-330 B.C.

Actual size approx. 18 mm

A coin of mythical beauty and rarity, this coin had one auction appearance: in Paris in 1985 at a Vinchon sale, where it brought 33,000 French francs. When one of these again comes to market, if it is in Extremely Fine or better with no problems it could easily surpass $200,000.

Tarentum was the largest and richest of the Greek colonies on the Italian peninsula, but by the late fourth century B.C. the city was in trouble from fierce Italic tribes from the mountains. The Greeks lacked the resources to resist the tribes without help. The reverse of this coin depicts their predicament in mythical terms: it shows Taras, the eponymous founder of Tarentum, asking the help of his father Poseidon, representing Alexander of Epirus (the uncle of Alexander the Great).

The reverse of this stater bears a complex scene without numismatic precedent.

Gold was seldom used by Greek cities except in times of crisis, and these staters were used as payment to Alexander and his troops. Although Alexander of Epirus was initially victorious over the Italic tribes, he proved to be more interested in building his own power than in aiding Tarentum, and the alliance began to break up. Weakened by defections, Alexander was defeated and killed in 331 B.C. at the Battle of Pandosia, on the banks of the Acheron. This significant battle discouraged further Greek colonization in Italy and may even have prevented Alexander the Great

from attempting to conquer it. The battle also saw one of the few failures of the Greeks' hugely successful phalanx formation, and Roman troops would later turn the winning tactics of the Italic warriors to their own use.

The obverse of this coin bears the head of Hera, wife of Zeus, wearing a decorated stephane (tiara), a veil, an earring, and a necklace. To the left is the letter E, and to the right are a dolphin and the first letters of the city's name. Hera is rendered much more delicately than usual on this die.

The reverse is the more powerful and tender side of this great coin. Poseidon, seated, holds a trident, and on his lap rests a bow. Coming toward him is the nude boy Taras, Poseidon's son by the nymph Satyrion, who appeals to his father with outstretched arms. The name of the city appears in the left field, while the artist's initial K is under the throne with a star in the right field. It is a complex scene without numismatic precedent and was executed by the same hand as the obverse.

This issue is universally regarded as one of the finest of all Greek dies.

ALEXANDER THE GREAT TETRADRACHM

GREECE · 336-323 B.C.

Actual size approx. 27 mm

Alexander the Great tetradrachms exist in the tens of thousands of examples, but there are at least that many people who want to own one, for obvious reasons. They used to cost $25 in the 1960s, rising to $150 in the 1970s and $300 in the 1980s. Today Extremely Fine or better coins cost between $700 and $1,200. The example described here is worth about $3,000 today, although specimens of this type are rarely available. In fact, in more than 40 years of dealing in ancient coins the author has never handled one.

The coinage of Alexander the Great, primarily the silver tetradrachm, is one of the most important issues of the entire Greek period. The obverse bears an anepigraphic image of a beardless, youthful Hercules wearing a lion's scalp. On the reverse is a partially draped Zeus seated on a throne, holding a staff in his left hand and an eagle that faces him in his right. The reverse legend reads, "of Alexander" or "of King Alexander." Various symbols in the reverse field indicate where the coin was minted and sometimes the exact year of its creation.

Until the discovery of what is thought to be the tomb of Alexander's father, Philip II of Macedonia, we did not know with absolute certainty what Alexander looked like. As noted earlier, in Philip's tomb at Vergina were two small ivory portraits of Philip and Alexander. The beardless portrait on Alexander's tetradrachms is strikingly similar to the portrait of Alexander found in his father's tomb. Additionally, the sarcophagus of Abdalonymos, known also as the Alexander Sarcophagus, shows Alexander on horseback wearing a lion's skin, like the Hercules figure on Alexander's tetradrachm. Abdalonymos, the last king of Sidon, was a personal friend of Alexander the Great and dedicated his sarcophagus to Alexander and himself. Moreover, a tetradrachm struck by the Bactrian king Agathocles in 171 to 160 B.C. bears a portrait of a beardless young man wearing a lion's skin—similar to

that on Alexander's own tetradrachm——and bears the legend "Alexander Son of King Philip." These facts make it clear that the tetradrachms of Alexander bear the actual portrait of the first man to conquer the known world.

The earliest tetradrachms of Alexander struck at Pella and Amphipolis are the sources of the most realistic and personal portraits of the young king. Except for his earliest coins, struck in Macedonia, the coinage of Alexander is made from silver that he captured in his conquest of the known world. This silver was turned into coins to pay the soldiers who were with him during the famous campaign that led him all the way to Afghanistan. Some of the coins, especially those minted in Babylon, were made from silver that most likely came from Persepolis, the treasury of Darius, the great Persian king defeated by Alexander. The most beautiful Alexander tetradrachms, some bearing a rose symbol, were struck during Alexander's lifetime at the Memphis mint in Egypt.

The tetradrachm of Alexander the Great became the international world currency, replacing the Athenian tetradrachm. They were minted widely, at as many as 75 mints, from 336 B.C. until about 70 B.C. The later posthumous issues are struck on a broader planchet than are issues of Alexander's early lifetime, but are always between 17.2 and 16.8 grams in weight. All bear the portrait of one of the greatest kings and conquerors history has ever recorded.

CORINTH STATER

GREECE · CIRCA 330-300 B.C.

Actual size approx. 23 mm

These coins used to cost $50 in the 1960s and $250 in the 1980s. Now Extremely Fine coins bring $500 to $800, unless they have unusual symbols or are in wonderful condition.

Corinth, one of the most important Greek city-states, was located on the narrow isthmus connecting the Peloponnesus to the Greek mainland. It controlled land routes north and south between the Peloponnesus and the mainland, and a specially constructed "ship road" enabled ships to be hauled across the narrow isthmus, avoiding the long trip around the Peloponnesus. Corinth made money from all the trade that passed through its territory, and the Corinthians themselves became leading merchants throughout the eastern Mediterranean. Corinth was one of the first cities of the Greek mainland to adopt coinage, and from the beginning the obverse type of her staters, the largest silver denomination, was the Pegasos. Corinth was associated with many myths, particularly those about the flying horse and Bellerophon, the hero who tamed him. Above the city of Corinth stood the Acrocorinthos, a massive rocky mountain. According to myth, high on a cliff on that mountain the Pegasos struck its hoof, leaving an enormous horseshoe-shaped impression in the rock that can still be seen today, and from that indentation in the rock a famous spring flows.

The reverse of these staters at first had only a punch mark, but that was soon replaced by the head of a lovely woman wearing a helmet. The head was long identified as Athena, but is now recognized as an armed Aphrodite, the chief goddess of the city. There was a famous temple of Aphrodite, the goddess of love, on the Acrocorinthos, and the long and winding road up to it was lined with establishments catering to those who worshipped the goddess. Corinth was the favorite port for ancient Greek sailors on leave.

In addition to the head of armed Aphrodite, a symbol, a monogram, or several letters appear on the reverse, usually behind Aphrodite's head. These identified the magistrates responsible for a particular issue of coins.

The Corinthian staters are among the most attractive and economically important Greek coins.

During the fourth century, the "colts" of Corinth, as its silver staters were called, became an international currency, circulating widely in the Greek world. Almost 30 colonies established by Corinth, primarily in western Greece, issued staters identical to those of Corinth except for the initials of the cities' names, which appeared under the Pegasos on the obverse. The Corinthian staters are among the most attractive and economically important Greek coins. The staters of Corinth and her colonies are sometimes found in Sicily and southern Italy, where they traveled in trade, primarily to pay for grain imports from that region to the Greek mainland.

650 B.C.   450   250   50 | 50   250   450   650   850   1050   1250   1450 A.D.

ALEXANDER THE GREAT PORUS DECADRACHM

GREECE · CIRCA 327 B.C.

Actual size approx. 36 mm

This is one of the most spectacular and historic coins in numismatics, but very few exist and none of them are perfectly struck—although this does not deter any buyers. The specimen discussed here was sold for $30,000 in the early 1990s. In the Gemini II sale, held in early 2006, it sold for over $100,000, and today it would bring even more.

One of the greatest numismatic rarities and mysteries is the Porus decadrachm of Alexander the Great. King Porus ruled Paurava, one of the many Indian kingdoms invaded by Alexander in his offensive against Persia. Unlike neighboring rulers, Porus was determined to resist the conqueror, and he prepared an army complete with war elephants to defend his kingdom against the Macedonian forces. The two armies met at the battle of the Hydaspes river, which would be Alexander's last major battle. Casualties were extensive on both sides, and although Alexander ultimately vanquished Porus's army, his exhausted troops refused to penetrate further into India. When asked by Alexander what penalty should be imposed upon him, Porus replied only that he wished to be treated in a manner befitting a king. This response, as well as Porus's fierce defense of his kingdom, won the Macedonian warrior's respect, and he allowed Porus to continue as ruler of his own people. Respect ripened into friendship, and Porus eventually joined in alliance with Alexander.

The traditional understanding of this type is that it represents Alexander on his famous horse Bucephalus, attacking Porus. In recent years a number of scholars have suggested other explanations, but none of these has garnered a large following. The decadrachms were most likely struck either during Alexander's campaign against Porus or as awards and presentation pieces immediately after Porus was defeated at the battle of the Hydaspes River in 327 B.C.

On the obverse of this large coin we see a horseman thrusting a long spear at a warrior riding on an elephant and grasping at the spear. A second warrior, the mahout, brandishes a spear and holds two more in reserve. There is a single Greek letter in the upper field. The reverse shows a standing figure, presumably Alexander, holding a thunderbolt and a long spear, being crowned by a flying Nike, the goddess of victory. Alexander wears oriental garb rather than traditional Greek clothing, which would indicate an orientalization of the conqueror. There is a small monogram in the field.

> The Porus decadrachm marks the easternmost advance of Alexander and is the only departure from his standard coin types.

The Porus decadrachm marks the easternmost advance of Alexander and is the only departure from his standard coin types. Only about 10 specimens of this rare coin are recorded. There is also a parallel series of tetradrachms featuring an archer on the obverse and an Indian elephant on the reverse. A second type in this series shows a quadriga; at present, only one such coin is known.

650 B.C. 450 250 50 50 250 450 650 850 1050 1250 1450 A.D.

Actual size approx. 30 mm

Although these coins are not at all rare, in the 1970s and 1980s an excellent example would bring SFr 2,000. Recently a great Mint State coin brought 20,000 euros, but that was unusual. Really good Mint State examples bring $3,000 or more, but nice Very Fines run $750. Late posthumous broad-flan coins cost up to $1,200 in Mint State.

After the death of Alexander the Great in 323 B.C., his generals turned upon one another in hopes of securing at least a piece of his empire for themselves. One of the most long-lived of these generals was Lysimachus, who had once served in Alexander's personal guard. He became the king of Thrace and eventually gained control of Macedonia, Thessaly, and much of western Anatolia before he was killed in a battle against Seleucus in 281 B.C.

Lysimachus's coinage does not become outstanding until 297 to 281 B.C., when he issued gold staters, silver tetradrachms, and silver drachms bearing the portrait of Alexander the Great. The workmanship varies from mint to mint and die to die, but the great majority of pieces are well executed and some, like the specimen shown here, rise to the level of high art.

With this coin Lysimachus emphasizes his connection with Alexander and his ideals, and provides us with our finest numismatic image of the great conqueror. The obverse shows Alexander in idealized form, although still retaining enough of his own features to be instantly recognizable. His gaze is raised heavenward and there is an element of pathos in his expression, perhaps a reflection of his young life cut short. As befits a king, he wears the royal diadem, as well as the ram's horn of Ammon. As pharaoh of Egypt, Alexander was regarded there as the son of Ammon, whom the Greeks equated with Zeus, king of the gods. Olympias,

Alexander's mother, had long claimed that Zeus was Alexander's true father, rather than Philip, her husband, whom she often quarreled with and periodically tried to murder. The reverse shows Athena with her weaponry seated on a throne holding a statuette of Nike, the goddess of victory, that crowns Lysimachus's name. The figure of Athena is both powerful and calm. The statuette of Nike she holds appears to be conferring victory on Lysimachus. The inscription reads, "King Lysimachus." The symbols in the field before Athena and in the exergue are mint control marks.

With this coin Lysimachus provides us with our finest numismatic image of the great conqueror.

Because they were a recognized and reliable currency, gold staters and tetradrachms bearing Lysimachus's types continued to be issued by a variety of mints long after his death. The quality of these later Lysimachoi, as they were called, tends to be mediocre and spiritless. The last examples, coined at Byzantium in the first century B.C., owed more to Celtic art than to Greek, and are truly bizarre.

650 B.C.   450   250   50   50   250   450   650   850   1050   1250   1450 A.D.

DEMETRIUS POLIORCETES
TETRADRACHM WITH NIKE ON PROW
GREECE · CIRCA 294 B.C.

Actual size approx. 29 mm

In the 1960s the price for these coins was SFr 1,950; in the 1970s, SFr 7,000; and in 1981 one brought $8,500. In the mid-1990s a large group of Mint State coins came to the market at $2,000 each. The prices are slightly higher now, but not by much. Within a few years the fact that a hoard ever existed will be forgotten, and the prices will go back to where they were.

Of all the contending generals who fought to claim Alexander's empire, none was more colorful than Demetrius Poliorcetes, who in the course of his career came close to conquering all of the empire. The son of Alexander's general Antigonus I Monophthalmus ("the One-Eyed"), he became known as the Besieger of Cities because of his famous attempts, mostly unsuccessful, to conquer Rhodes and several other notable cities. The war maker transformed the renowned temple of Athena, the Parthenon in Athens, into his private residence, complete with a harem of considerable size.

Demetrius's coinage, like his life, is notable for its originality.

Demetrius Poliorcetes was born to Antigonus Gonatas and his wife Stratonice in 336 B.C., the same year Alexander the Great came to power. In 321 he married Phila, the daughter of Antipater. In 313 he was appointed governor of Syria and Phoenicia, but the next year he was defeated by Ptolemy I at the battle of Gaza. In 307, having freed Athens from Cassander, he and his father were hailed as "savior gods" by the people of Athens. In 306 Demetrius laid siege to Salamis in Cyprus, defeating Ptolemy, and received the title of king. Three years later, after numerous victories, he was hailed commander-in-chief of the allied Hellenic states.

In 301 B.C., Antigonus was killed by the forces of his old comrades-in-arms, Lysimachus and Seleucus, at the battle of Ipsus. Demetrius escaped and four years later formed an alliance with Seleucus. Wars continued one after another until Lysimachus, Seleucus, Ptolemy, and Pyrrhus formed a new alliance against Demetrius. At this point large numbers of Macedonians deserted him, and in 288 he was defeated and fled to Greece. Here he raised another army, which met with both failure and (less frequently) success. Finally Seleucus defeated Demetrius in 285 and placed him in honorable captivity in Syria, where he died in 282 at the age of 46.

Demetrius's coinage, like his life, is notable for its originality. This is particularly true of his fine tetradrachms that feature on the obverse a winged Nike standing on the prow of a ship. She blows a trumpet and holds a naval standard, the symbol of victory. The reverse shows a magnificent standing Poseidon wielding a trident, as seen from the back. The coin recalls two important Greek statuary works: the magnificent Victory of Samothrace (seen on the ship's prow), and the great bronze Poseidon recovered from the sea and now in the Athens museum.

Actual size approx. 62 mm

Many of these coins come from a single 19th-century find, so most of them have an excellent green patination and are in Extremely Fine condition. They cost $1,000 in the 1970s and $2,000 in the 1990s; now they bring $3,500.

At the beginning of 289 B.C., the Roman people possessed vigor, social organization, a force of 273,000 eligible farmer-citizen soldiers, and a leadership driven to rule as many lands as possible. At this time, Rome's wealth derived primarily from agriculture. Some people grew grapes, olives, and other fruit, while others raised cattle, sheep, and pigs. Although all of these products were useful for bartering, they were perishable, so a coinage system became necessary. This gave rise to the advent of cast-bronze coins. An *as* equaled a pound of bronze, and could be used to buy wine, wheat, or a few days' lodging. A wealthy man might have a net worth of 100,000 *asses*. In contrast, a poor man might hold less than 15,000.

The obverse of the *as* depicts a laureate head of Janus, one of the earliest of the Roman gods, whose two faces signify knowledge of the past and the future.

In the ancient world, precious-metal coinage was struck to exacting standards of purity and weight, at least during periods of economic prosperity and political stability. The value of a gold, silver, or electrum coin was based upon the value of the metal it contained. Ancient Greek bronze coinage was, from its introduction at the close of the fifth century B.C., a token coinage with a trade value greater than the worth of its metal. The earliest Roman base-metal coinage followed yet another pattern, consisting of enormous cast-bronze pieces roughly valued at their weight in metal. Most typical of these is the aes grave *as* (literally, "heavy bronze *as*"), weighing slightly less than a Roman pound, and its accompanying fractional coinage.

The casting of the aes grave *as* began around 289 B.C. After 225 B.C., the obverse of the *as* depicted a laureate head of Janus, one of the earliest of the Roman gods, whose two faces signified knowledge of the past and the future. He is similar to the god Helios because he is related to the sun, beginning and ending each day. Janus was the god through whom all other gods were reached, and he saved the Romans from the Sabines. The temple of Janus, depicted on coins of Nero, glorified war and was closed during times of peace. The reverse shows the prow of a ship facing right, with the mark of value "I" (indicating one *as*) above it. These first Janus *asses* averaged around 268 grams, but their weight rapidly fell; by 217 B.C. the average weight was only 132 grams. Well-preserved examples of the early, heavy Janus aes grave *asses* are readily available, and all probably come from one find from the 19th century since they have the same green patination.

650 B.C. 450 250 50 50 250 450 650 850 1050 1250 1450 A.D.

Actual size approx. 18 mm

The only time one of these coins has ever come up for public sale was at a Bank Leu sale in Zurich in May 1991, when an about Extremely Fine specimen brought SFr 42,900. Since then a very small group has come onto the market, all in Mint State condition, with sales at above $100,000.

Pergamon, located in what is now western Turkey, was one of the richest cities of Hellenistic times. It was part of the empire of Alexander the Great, who seized the region from the Persians, and it was made great by Philetaerus (282–263 B.C.), who during the wars of Alexander's successors first served Antigonus, then Lysimachus, and then finally Seleucus I. After the death of Seleucus, Philetaerus became independent and gained control of the considerable treasury that had once belonged to Seleucus. Under his leadership, the city became a center of wealth, art, literature, sophistication, and considerable military power. It was famous for its cult of Asclepius, the demigod of healing, which was established in the early fourth century B.C., as well as for its altar's magnificent marble frieze, 390 feet long and 7.5 feet high, which now resides in the Pergamon Museum in Berlin. The altar was discovered in 1878 by archeologist Karl Humann: it had been built into a Byzantine wall as if it were no more than old stones, and pagan ones at that.

These exquisite gold staters were produced at Pergamon, most likely early in the reign of Alexander. The obverse features a head of Alexander as Hercules, wearing a lion skin. This is the same type used on Alexander's silver decadrachms, tetradrachms, and drachms, but only in this issue does the type appear in gold. We now know the portrait is of Alexander, not only from the ivory portrait of him found in his father's tomb at Vergina, but also because of the portrayal of Alexander on the tomb of his friend Abdalonymus, king of Sidon. A panel of the tomb, which is now in the Istanbul Archaeology Museum, shows a scene from the battle of Issus in 333 B.C., and in it Alexander is portrayed wearing the lion skin while riding his horse Bucephalus.

The reverse is equally wonderful. It is the only gold coin that features the famous Palladium of Troy. This image of Athena was regarded as the guardian of Troy, and tradition held that the city could never be taken as long as the Palladium remained in Troy. According to mythology, the Greek heroes Diomedes and Odysseus entered the city through a secret passage and removed the Palladium, thus making it possible for the Greeks to get the Trojan Horse into the city and win the war. According to other myths, the Palladium subsequently made its way to Athens, Argos, or Sparta, but the most common story is that it was not taken from Troy at all until the fall of the city, when the Trojan hero Aeneas rescued it and carried it with Trojan refugees to Italy. Aeneas's descendants founded Rome, and the Palladium, now regarded as the guardian of Rome, was deposited in the temple of Vesta in the Roman Forum. The Palladium is often depicted on Roman coinage held by the emperor, but it is never shown as clearly or in such detail as on this coin of Pergamon.

Athena and her Palladium were important to Alexander, who claimed descent from Achilles, the great Greek hero of the Trojan War and a favorite of the goddess. A head of Athena graces the obverse of every one of Alexander's gold staters, although this is the only Alexander-related gold coin with a complete figure of Athena.

This issue is quite remarkable in that it uses major motifs and types of Alexander's coinage but in a way that they were never used elsewhere in gold. It is also remarkable because it relates to Troy, Alexander the Great, and the Roman empire and its founding, all in one coin. Until a very small group of these coins came to light, only four were recorded, with three in museums. They remain very rare, unique to type, and relevant to all.

650 B.C.   450   250   50   50   250   450   650   850   1050   1250   1450 A.D.

ARSINOË II GOLD OCTODRACHM

EGYPT · BEGINNING 270-269 B.C.

Actual size approx. 28 mm

These magnificent coins usually come in Mint State condition unless they have been used in jewelry. In 1959 one sold for SFr 3,000, but by the 1970s they commanded SFr 20,000. They then dropped to $6,000 and now sell for $12,500. The issue with a K in back of the queen's head is the most common and stylistically not as good or valuable as earlier issues.

Most Greek mints struck little gold, and then mainly small coins. This gold eight-drachm coin is an exception, having been struck in Egypt to honor Arsinoë II, sister and wife of Ptolemy II of Egypt.

During the series of wars that followed the death of Alexander the Great, his general Ptolemy secured Egypt for himself and established a dynasty there that ruled for nearly three centuries. His was the last of the Hellenistic Greek dynasties to fall to Rome, upon the death of the famous Cleopatra VII in 30 B.C.

Royal family life during the Hellenistic period was complex and filled with intrigue. The various royal houses were all integrated, but that did not prevent them from constantly scheming against one another. Plotting wars and murders was common.

> A hint of Egypt's vast wealth can be seen in this coin, which is much larger and heavier than most Greek gold coins.

Arsinoë II was the daughter of Ptolemy I. Her first marriage was to Lysimachus, king of Thrace. After his death in battle she was briefly forced into marriage with her stepbrother, Ptolemy Graunus. Fleeing from this arrangement, she returned to Egypt, where she married her brother, Ptolemy II. Brother-sister marriages were not common in Egypt at that time, but since Ptolemy was absolute ruler of Egypt *and* a living god (at least according to Egyptian tradition), he could do as he pleased.

The years of the joint reign of Ptolemy II and Arsinoë II were the most brilliant in the three centuries of the dynasty. They controlled vast areas beyond Egypt, including Palestine, the Greek mainland, and portions of Anatolia. The Ptolemaic fleet dominated the Mediterranean. The rulers' court glittered, attracting the finest literary figures, architects, and artists. The famous Library of Alexandria and the Museum of Alexandria, a center for scientific study, were established at this time. Egypt was at its richest.

A hint of Egypt's vast wealth can be seen in this coin, which is much larger and heavier than most Greek gold coins. On the obverse is a portrait of the middle-aged Arsinoë II. She appears regal rather than beautiful, wearing a diadem and, modestly, a veil draped over her head.

The reverse shows a double cornucopia bound by a ribbon. At the top of the cornucopia are grains of wheat with fruit and grapes dangling from the edges. The type refers to the agricultural wealth of Egypt, a major exporter of grain throughout the Mediterranean. The Greek legend surrounding the reverse reads, "Arsinoë who loves her brother," presented without the slightest hint of embarrassment.

650 B.C.　450　250　50　50　250　450　650　850　1050　1250　1450 A.D.

PTOLEMY III DYNASTIC OCTODRACHM

EGYPT · 246-221 B.C.

Actual size approx. 27 mm

This spectacular coin always comes with an area of dullness at the highest point of the relief, which is the king's hair. The price was $5,000 in the 1960s, which rose to $15,000 in the 1990s, then dropped back to $5,000 in the late '90s when a number of specimens came on the market. The price has now recovered to $12,500.

Continuity and legitimacy were of major importance to the Greek dynasts who ruled the kingdoms that grew out of the breakup of Alexander the Great's empire. On this coin, Ptolemy III (246–221 B.C.) advertises his ancestors. On one side we see the founder of the dynasty, Ptolemy I, the general of Alexander who had established control over Egypt and a number of adjacent areas, and his wife, Berenike I. Above their heads is the Greek word for "gods." Both had been deified in accordance with pre-Greek Egyptian tradition and the pragmatic needs of dynastic politics. On the other side we see the busts of Ptolemy II and his sister and wife Arsinoë II. Above their heads is the Greek word for "siblings." While modern mores prohibit incestuous marriage between brother and sister, it was at least permissible in late Egyptian culture, and became common among Egyptian monarchs. Certainly no one would have objected openly to a powerful and absolute ruler such as Ptolemy III, the child of the siblings' union.

The first coins of this type may have actually been issued by Ptolemy II, but they certainly continued to be struck throughout the reign of Ptolemy III and perhaps beyond. It is interesting to see the portraits of both Ptolemy I, the field-hardened general, and Ptolemy II, his aristocratic son.

It is notable that this is a large gold coin, an octodrachm. Ancient Egypt was rich in gold, and this high-value coin would have advertised the somewhat perverse dynasty of the Ptolemys only to those who mattered in the kingdom—the rich and powerful.

It is estimated that more than 2,000 of these great coins still exist.

This coin would have advertised the dynasty of the Ptolemys only to those who mattered in the kingdom—the rich and powerful.

650 B.C.   450   250   50   50   250   450   650   850   1050   1250   1450 A.D.

BERENIKE II DODECADRACHM OR PENTADECADRACHM

EGYPT · CIRCA 241 B.C.

Actual size approx. 34 mm

When these came to market in the mid-1990s there were originally thought to exist only one or two, and at that time they sold for $200,000. As more came out, the prices dropped, until they stabilized at their present value of $25,000. Most of the less than 50 coins have cracks from striking, and the depth of the crack has a direct bearing on the small fluctuations in value.

The family history of Egypt's Ptolemaic dynasty was complex and resembles a soap opera. The third king, Ptolemy III, came to the throne in 246 B.C. and later married his cousin Berenike (II). When war broke out with the rival Seleucid kingdom, Ptolemy III went off to run the army, leaving Berenike II to run the government. She was a strong woman, both in personality and physically. In her younger days she had driven chariots in competition and won, and she was also the subject of a famous poem, "The Lock of Berenike," by Callimachus.

This extraordinary woman is depicted on the obverse of the second-largest silver coin struck in antiquity, weighing about 52 grams. (The largest is a silver medallion of an obscure Indo-Greek ruler, known from four specimens.)

Why was such an immense coin ever created? No one knows for sure.

On the obverse Berenike wears a veil over her head, and just the edge of a royal diadem can be seen peeking beyond the veil. Her hair is elaborately curled, and her features are much the same as those of other early Ptolemaic queens.

On the reverse is a beribboned cornucopia overflowing with grain and fruit, indicative of the agricultural wealth of Egypt. In the field flanking the cornucopia are the two caps of the Dioscuri, young male deities worshipped by the royal house. The legend proclaims, "Queen Berenike."

The denomination the coin represents is a matter of controversy. It was long considered a 12-drachma coin on the Attic weight standard, but one numismatist has recently argued that it is a 15-drachma piece on the Egyptian standard. In any event, such a coin was much too valuable for everyday commerce.

Why was such an immense coin ever created? No one knows for sure, but there are several plausible theories. The coins may have been struck for the dowry of Berenike II and the festivities and expenses that surrounded the royal wedding. Or the coins may have been coined out of the Seleucid war booty, which seems to have been great. During the war, Ptolemy III occupied the Seleucid capitol, which he thoroughly looted, and also acquired rich ports in Palestine and Syria. The annual revenue of one of these ports alone was equal to a tenth of the immense total of government revenues from all of Egypt.

In 1904, when J. N. Svoronos's standard study of Ptolemaic coinage was published, only one example of this coin was known, and it was broken. Since then, about 40 examples have come to light, a number of which are also broken.

HANNIBAL COIN

Actual size approx. 25 mm

This coin has no auction appearances in recent history, although an example from the famous Richard Cyril Lockett collection sold in London in 1955 for £1,070. Today that coin would bring well over $100,000.

Of all the great military figures in the ancient world, three stand out above all others: Alexander the Great, Julius Caesar, and the great Carthaginian leader Hannibal.

Following the long and costly first war against Rome (264–241 B.C.), Hannibal's father, General Hamilcar, died, and control of Carthaginian Spain passed to Hannibal. This coin was issued during the decade of 230 to 221 B.C., before the outbreak of the Second Punic War (221–204 B.C.). The figure on the obverse is Hannibal portrayed as Melqarth, who corresponded to the Greek god Hades, king of the Underworld. Numismatists have two reasons for believing that the portrait incorporates the features of a young Hannibal: first, prior to this coin, Melqarth was usually depicted as older and bearded; and second, the head displays some of Hannibal's individual features, such as his sideburns, his heavy brows, and his sharp nose. (It is known that when Hieronymus, the boy king of Syracuse, allied himself with Hannibal, he grew sideburns as well, as a sign of his allegiance.) The portrait wears the laurel wreath, as was appropriate for both gods and victorious generals.

The issue of this coin had probably ceased by the beginning of the Second Punic War in 218 B.C. and Hannibal's departure from Spain. From southern Spain, Hannibal's army marched north across the peninsula and over the Pyrenees into what is now southern France, ultimately crossing the rugged Alps and invading Italy from the north. It was an amazing feat, especially because along with his infantry he traveled with elephants, such as we see

depicted on the reverse of this coin, and a full baggage train. The war elephant was not only one of Carthage's most important weapons, but it also symbolized Africa, the Carthaginian homeland.

Numismatists have two reasons for believing that the portrait incorporates the features of a young Hannibal.

Hannibal waged war against Rome in Italy for more than a decade and a half, until the Roman general Scipio managed to invade North Africa and threaten the city of Carthage itself. Finally, in a battle at Zama, near Carthage, Hannibal's beloved war elephants stampeded at the wrong time, decimating his infantry. After the war, Hannibal fled Carthage to escape Roman wrath, but the Romans continued to hunt him until he committed suicide around 183 B.C. Nor did Carthage survive for long. Rome destroyed the city-state in 146 B.C.

650 B.C.   450   250   50   50   250   450   650   850   1050   1250   1450 A.D.

OATH-TAKING STATER

ROME · 218 B.C.

Actual size approx. 18 mm

In 1966 one specimen brought SFr 12,000; in the 1990s the going price was $40,000; and today they bring $100,000. These coins normally come in Very Fine condition.

Originally founded by the Phoenicians in North Africa, Carthage had become a major power by the middle of the third century B.C. With its vast wealth derived from its commercial activities, the city-state controlled much of the coast of North Africa and almost all of Spain. The First Punic War, in which Carthage and the expanding republic of Rome struggled for ascendancy, was fought from 264 to 241 B.C. It had cost Rome and Italy perhaps as many as 300,000 men and had settled nothing; both sides remained strong and resentful. The Second Punic War had broken out in 221, and Rome was clearly getting the worst of it. By 218 B.C. Italy itself was being invaded.

At the beginning of the Second Punic War, Hannibal, the Carthaginian general and one of the greatest military minds of antiquity, led his army of foot soldiers, cavalry, and elephants out of southern Spain, northward across the Pyrenees, east through what is now southern France, and over the Alps, and invaded Italy from the north. (Remarkably, though endowed with neither the physique nor the aptitude for Alpine expeditions, all of his elephants survived the trek.) Once in Italy, Hannibal destroyed one Roman legion after another. It was in this context that the first truly Roman gold coinage was struck.

Rome commissioned the coins, in stater and half-stater denominations, in an effort to pay the expenses of war, raise and supply new troops, and stave off Hannibal's attack. The obverse shows the janiform head of the Dioscuri. The head of Janus, the two-faced deity who presided over the beginning and end of things—and after whom our month of January is named—was the traditional type on many early Roman coins. Here the head has been given the features of the young twin brother gods known for bringing help in battle.

> Described as an oath-taking scene, the depiction shows soldiers at their swearing-in ceremony.

The reverse of the coin is more interesting. Traditionally described as an oath-taking scene, the depiction shows soldiers at their swearing-in ceremony. On the left, an officer stands, bearded and without armor, facing a young, unbearded, armor-clad recruit at the right. Between them kneels another soldier holding a sword and the pig that will be sacrificed after the taking of the military oath— a solemn and terrible vow, calling down the wrath of the gods on the oath-taker and his family should he fail to live up to his responsibilities. Roman soldiers, as well as those of allied communities, had been unnerved by Hannibal's bloody victories; this coin, with its simple inscription ROMA, served to remind them of their solemn oaths and obligations.

Hannibal ravaged Italy for 15 years until Rome finally defeated Carthage in 203 B.C., but the Romans never forgave or forgot. They provoked a third war with Carthage in 149 B.C., and utterly destroyed the city and its population three years later.

650 B.C.   450   250   50   50   250   450   650   850   1050   1250   1450 A.D.

40-AS GOLD COIN

ROME · 211 B.C.

Actual size approx. 11 mm

There are only 11 of these coins recorded. In 1968 at a Hess-Leu sale one brought SFr 8,900. In the Triton III sale in 1999 one sold for $36,000. None have come up for sale since then, but when one does it will greatly surpass that price.

In 211 B.C., Rome was in the middle of the Second Punic War, the greatest war in its history. The First Punic War had been bad enough. Fought largely at sea, it resulted in more naval dead than all the maritime casualties of World War I and World War II combined. The second war, again between Rome and Carthage, broke out in 221 and lasted until 203 B.C. The conflict was widespread. Large stretches of the Italian countryside that were productive farmlands before that war became ruined wastelands due to repeated burnings and the onset of erosion. In addition to Italy, vicious fighting erupted in Spain, Sicily, Greece, and eventually North Africa, when the Romans ultimately carried the conflict into Carthage's homeland.

> As these gold coins were first being produced, the Romans also created a new silver denomination, the denarius.

By 211 B.C., the Romans finally had some success in this long war. Hannibal still ravaged Italy, but Roman forces had conquered Sicily. This was the context for the issue of the only sizable release of gold coins struck by Rome until the closing years of the republic, 150 years later. These were 60-*as*, 40-*as*, and 20-*as* coins, the *as* being the republican unit of value. All three denominations bear the same types. The obverse portrays the head of Mars facing right, bearded and wearing a Corinthian helmet. The reverse depicts an eagle standing right on a thunderbolt, below which is the inscription ROMA. A downward arrow (meaning 50), followed by X (10), indicates the denomination of the 60-*as* piece. The smaller denominations are specified by XXXX and XX. The workmanship on these small coins is excellent. It is likely that the Romans employed Greek die cutters.

As these gold coins were first being produced, the Romans also created a new silver denomination, the denarius. The denarius endured for centuries to become perhaps the most successful silver denomination of all time. Production of the gold coins, however, ceased after only a few years. A fair number of the 60-*as* and 20-*as* pieces survive today, most of them discovered in a few sizable hoards. The 40-*as* denomination is the great rarity, presumably struck in relatively small quantities, with only 11 recorded.

650 B.C.   450   250   50 | 50   250   450   650   850   1050   1250   1450 A.D.

FLAMININUS GOLD STATER

ROME · 187 B.C.

Actual size approx. 20 mm

Fewer than 10 of these coins are recorded. In the Triton III sale in 1999 an Extremely Fine specimen brought $253,000. A year later, a coin with some damage sold for $50,000, and the same coin sold in 2006 for the equivalent of $290,000.

By 200 B.C., Rome had won the Second Punic War against Carthage and had virtually turned the western Mediterranean into a Roman lake. Every shore was controlled by Rome, by Rome's allies, or by groups reduced to impotence by Rome's might. In the eastern Mediterranean, however, large Greek kingdoms still dominated, and Rome had a quarrel with one of those kingdoms. In northern Greece, Macedonia had allied with Carthage against Rome during the recent war, and now Rome was embroiled in a war against Macedonia.

At first the conflict progressed slowly, each side appearing to fear the other. Alexander the Great had emerged from Macedonia to conquer most of the known world, and even more than a century later Macedonian soldiers still had the reputation of being the most formidable in the Greek world. Moreover, because Macedonia dominated most of the city-states in southern Greece, it could draw upon those resources and also recruit mercenaries from the numerous Thracian tribes to its north and east. Nevertheless, even though Italy had been physically wasted by the war with Carthage, the Romans had a battle-hardened army whose tactics were unfamiliar to the Macedonians. For several years the adversaries circled one another warily until 198, when Rome commissioned a vigorous commander, Titus Quinctius Flamininus, who won victory for Rome in a climactic, decisive battle.

The Greeks anticipated their fate with apprehension, but Rome appeared to have no territorial ambitions in the eastern Mediterranean. It came as a complete surprise when Flamininus, appearing at the Isthmian Games at Corinth in 196, declared the Greek city-states free and independent—even from the influence of Macedonia. He also announced the withdrawal of Roman forces. The crowd at the games was so amazed that, according to Greek writers, they sent up a shout of joy so thunderous that it killed several crows flying overhead!

Unfortunately, the high idealism of Rome's withdrawal did not long endure. The Greeks were perpetually feuding and various factions continually attempted to involve the Romans in their disputes. Moreover, few Roman politicians were as principled as Flamininus. In the next 150 years, Rome would intervene repeatedly until the eastern Mediterranean, too, became part of their Roman lake. It was in this context that the gold stater of Flamininus was issued.

This stater is a remarkable departure from all previous and subsequent Roman coins. During the republic, Rome seldom struck gold coins. Furthermore, no living Roman had ever before been depicted on a coin, and none would be again until the time of Julius Caesar, some 150 years later. The obverse of the coin displays a portrait of Flamininus, finely executed in a remarkably realistic style and, unlike the diademed portraits of the Hellenistic Greek monarchs, bareheaded. On the reverse, Nike holds a palm branch, the symbol of victory, as she crowns his abbreviated name, T. QVINCTI, with a laurel wreath.

Fewer than 10 examples of the Flamininus stater are known, several of which were found in southern Italy and Sicily, probably carried there by returning soldiers.

PHARNACES I OF PONTUS TETRADRACHM

GREECE · 185/3–170 B.C.

Actual size approx. 32 mm

In 1968 a worn coin brought SFr 3,800, in 1988 a great coin went for SFr 48,000, and in 1978 the price was $37,400. Today a great coin would bring $50,000 to $60,000, but a worn one only $15,000.

The kingdom of Pontus, which lay in northern Anatolia on the shore of the Black Sea, had been part of the Persian Empire until the conquest of Alexander in 330 B.C. By the time this coin was minted, the royal house had become a mix of Greek and Persian bloodlines. Its members claimed direct descent from the Achaemenid dynasty of Persia, and thus from the demigod Perseus, ancestor of the Persian people. Since Perseus was the son of Zeus himself, the rulers of Pontus believed themselves to have the most distinguished of all bloodlines. The reality, however, was less lofty. Pontus was actually a poor kingdom, relatively small and remote, with few cities and a peasant population that was uneducated and hard to govern. The kingdom was often threatened by attacks from neighboring kingdoms, nearby Greek city-states, and marauding tribes.

This is a surprisingly elegant coin to have been issued by a relative backwater of the Greek world.

The chief interest in this coin is the diademed portrait of Pharnaces I, king of Pontus from 185 to 170 B.C., on its obverse. By the beginning of the third century B.C., portraits of living men had begun to appear on Greek coinage. Many of these likenesses were idealized interpretations, sometimes bearing little resemblance to the individual being portrayed. Hellenistic portraiture, however, was sometimes fully realistic and could, on exceptional occasions, go beyond realism to produce a psychologically insightful portrait. One such rarity is this head of Pharnaces I of Pontus. Pharnaces' self-image is expressed in the royal diadem and the artfully arranged hair. The king's face, however, shows him as a tough thug, thereby exposing the reality.

Although as carefully executed as the obverse, the reverse of the coin is somewhat mysterious. The standing male figure holds a cornucopia and a caduceus in one hand, and in the other a vine branch on which a young deer feeds. Each object represents an attribute of a specific Greek god. The cornucopia invokes Tyche, goddess of good fortune; the caduceus of Hermes brings spiritual awakening; joy springs from the ivy of Dionysus; and the stag belongs to Artemis, goddess of the hunt (but may also represent Perseus as a solar deity assimilating the characteristics of the other four). Three monograms in the field indicate the names of mint officials, while the star and crescent form the symbol of the royal house of Pontus. The inscription reads, "King Pharnakes."

Overall, this is a surprisingly elegant coin to have been issued by a relative backwater of the Greek world. Clearly, Pharnaces I employed a highly skilled die cutter who produced a true masterpiece.

PERSEUS "ZOILOS" SILVER TETRADRACHM

GREECE · CIRCA 178-173 B.C.

Actual size approx. 34 mm

In 1958 one of these coins sold for SFr 430, but by 1965 the price was SFr 3,000, and in 1982 one sold for $20,000. That price, however, was an anomaly, and specimens sold in 1985 for 15,000 deutsche marks and in 1989 for SFr 12,500. Today an Extremely Fine coin is worth $20,000.

Perseus was the last independent king to rule Macedonia. The son of Philip V, he made his way to the throne in 179 B.C. by doing in his older brother, Demetrius. His massive high-relief portrait as the new king of Macedonia graces the obverse of this coin. Also on the obverse, under the truncation of the neck, is the name ZOILOS in bold letters. Until recently scholars thought this to be the signature of the artist, but some now think it might be the name of a magistrate or a local governor. On the reverse, an oak wreath surrounds an eagle perched on a thunderbolt. Mint control marks and the king's name also appear on the reverse. There are only 20 Zoilos tetradrachms and one unique didrachm recorded. When compared to the rest of Perseus's portrait tetradrachms, the quality and rarity of the coins in this issue indicate that it must have been a coronation issue.

prevailed against Crassus, he was defeated and taken prisoner by L. Aemilius Paullus in 168.

Perseus was brought to Rome, where he was given the freedom of the city. He quickly adapted to his new surroundings and became part of fashionable society. He claimed to be much more content in Rome than he had been struggling with affairs of state in Macedonia. Nevertheless, in 62 B.C., a hundred years after the Macedonian downfall, L. Aemilius Lepidus Paullus issued a denarius commemorating that event with Perseus and his two sons depicted as captives on its reverse—a far cry from the godlike portrait on that long-ago coronation issue.

The quality and rarity of the coins in this issue indicate that it must have been a coronation issue.

The last several years of Perseus's reign were spent fighting off a Roman invasion that began with an attack led by P. Licinius Crassus in 171 B.C. He even enlisted the help of Rhodian mercenaries and struck Rhodian-type drachms to pay them. Although he

650 B.C.   450   250   50   50   250   450   650   850   1050   1250   1450 A.D.

EUCRATIDES I HEROIC BUST COIN

GREECE · CIRCA 171–145 B.C.

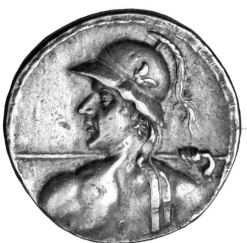

Actual size approx. 29 mm

These coins used to be worth $20,000 to $30,000 until a flood of coins came into the market in the middle 1990s and the price plummeted to $5,000. Today they are edging up to around $7,000. Most are Very Fine or better.

Late in the third century B.C., the Parthians, a native Persian dynasty, were able to wrest control of the area that is now modern Iran away from the Greek Seleucids, who had controlled it since the death of Alexander the Great and the breakup of his empire a century earlier. The Greeks who had settled in the far eastern portions of Alexander's empire found themselves cut off from their western brothers, and new Greek kings sprang up to rule these severed eastern lands, then called Bactria, now Afghanistan.

Regrettably, we know little about these eastern kings. Even though Eucratides was one of the most important among them, what is known about him would fill little more than a page. We do know that he came to the throne by defeating an earlier dynasty of eastern Greek kings and that he ruled in Bactria and western India. He may have been related to the Seleucids, the Greeks who ruled the areas of modern Syria and Iraq (and had once ruled all of the eastern lands originally conquered by Alexander). Our few surviving sources depict Eucratides as a vigorous and warlike ruler, fighting the Parthians to his west and advancing his control into India on the east. His death was undeserved, according to the late-Roman historian Justin, who relied on earlier sources now lost:

> As Eucratides returned from India, he was killed on the way back by his son, whom he had associated to his rule, and who, without hiding his parricide, as if he did not kill

a father but an enemy, ran with his chariot over the blood of his father, and ordered the corpse to be left without a sepulture. (Justin XLI, 6)

The impious son apparently did not rule in peace. There are indications that the kingdom soon fell into revolt and civil war. About 15 years after the assassination of Eucratides, nomadic tribes known as the Yueh-chih invaded from the north, and the weakened Greeks lost control of Bactria. They did, however, continue to rule in western India for nearly another century and a half.

Because the new kings wanted to legitimize their rule and proclaim their virtues, the coins struck by the eastern Greeks are often innovative in their design. On this coin Eucratides I, circa 171 to 145 B.C., is depicted as a heroic warrior. His bust is seen from behind and he is unclothed except for his helmet. During this period, nudity was used as an artistic convention designed to evoke images of heroic mythic warriors. The king's head is turned to his left, allowing us to observe his strong, almost severe face. Beneath his helmet he wears a royal diadem, as evidenced by the ribbons trailing down his well-muscled back, and like the heroes of old, he brandishes a mighty spear.

On the reverse the Dioscuri, Castor and Pollux, the patron gods of Eucratides, gallop right on spirited horses. They hold long spears and palms, the symbols of victory. The Greek inscription reads, "King, the Great Eucratides."

OROPHERNES SILVER TETRADRACHM

GREECE · CIRCA 161–159 B.C.

Actual size approx. 36 mm

These exquisite, extremely rare coins have never been cheap. In 1978 one brought SFr 130,000, and in the late 1980s one sold for $100,000. More recently, in the 2006 Gemini II sale, the final price was $82,800.

Cappadocia, a territory in the interior of Anatolia, now modern Turkey, was not a rich land. It was conquered by Cyrus in the middle of the sixth century B.C. and continued to be held by the Persians until their defeat by Alexander in 333 B.C. Although sometimes dominated by its more powerful neighbors, Cappadocia remained an independent monarchy from that time until its final king was deposed by the Romans. The kings of Cappadocia were closely related to the Seleucid dynasty that dominated Syria. Two Cappadocian kings, Ariarathes III and Ariarathes IV, married members of the Syrian royal family.

The tetradrachm of Orophernes, king of Cappadocia circa 161 to 159 B.C., is widely regarded as the most beautiful Hellenistic portrait coin. The obverse features an image of the young Orophernes wearing a royal diadem. On the reverse a winged Nike crowns his name, which reads, "King Orophernes the Victorious." In front of Nike is an owl on a small altar.

Clearly, Orophernes was a man of no small ego. Falsely claimed by his mother to be the son of King Ariarathes IV of Cappadocia, he was set on the throne as a puppet ruler by Demetrius I Soter, king of the Seleucid Empire in Syria, and proved to be totally incompetent. He enjoyed the pleasures of being a ruler but eschewed the work. In fact, he never actually won a victory and was a person of little historical importance. Within three years his own people had removed him from the throne.

Aware that his reign might be coming to an end, Orophernes took 400 talents from his people and gave them for safekeeping to the Ionian city of Priene. When Ariarathes V drove Orophernes out of Cappadocia and seized the throne, he demanded the return of the money; Priene refused to repay the 400 talents, so Ariarathes V and King Attalus of Pergamon sacked the city. Orophernes fled to Syria and supposed safety, where he began plotting against his patron Demetrius, who promptly had him executed.

> The tetradrachm of Orophernes is widely regarded as the most beautiful Hellenistic portrait coin.

Of the 10 Orophernes tetradrachms that are known, 9 were found in 1870 in a temple at Priene in Turkey. Two of these are broken and most of the others are now in museums.

650 B.C.   450   250   50   50   250   450   650   850   1050   1250   1450 A.D.

Actual size approx. 22 mm

In its few auction appearances this issue has always done well. In 1970 a fleur-de-coin (FDC) or perfect specimen brought SFr 21,000, and in 1975 one in Extremely Fine made SFr 51,000. The coin discussed here was purchased on December 16, 2003, for SFr 100,000. Today it would bring much more.

Gold was not a normal part of the monetary system of the Roman Republic. It was only occasionally issued, in times of crisis. One such issue was struck by Lucius Cornelius Sulla in 84 to 83 B.C. during his campaign against Mithradates the Great, king of Pontus.

The 80s B.C. were a disturbed time in the Mediterranean world. In the early years of the decade Italy was torn apart by a war between the Romans and their longtime Italian allies, over the question of citizenship. That war also revived factional strife within the Roman Republic between the aristocratic Senate that had long controlled the government and an opposition group that intended to take power into its own hands. At the same time, the ambitious Mithradates, ruler of a small kingdom in northern Anatolia (modern northern Turkey), took advantage of Rome's preoccupation with the problems closer to home to overrun the Roman province of Asia, which comprised western Anatolia. There, to tie the inhabitants more closely to his cause and prevent any defections to the Romans, Mithradates encouraged a mass slaughter of all Italians in Anatolia. Tens of thousands were murdered. Then Mithradates went on to invade mainland Greece itself.

Sulla, a member of the senatorial aristocracy, led an army to Greece to oppose Mithradates. Sulla defeated Mithradates in battle and then, after a harsh siege, captured his chief base, Athens, and drove Mithradates' forces out of Greece. He then followed Mithradates to Anatolia and defeated him there. Sulla was willing to extend relatively liberal terms to Mithradates, part of which was a large payment, because back in Italy the anti-senatorial faction had seized

control and sent an army east against Sulla. As it turned out, that army did not present much of a threat to Sulla. Much of it eventually defected and joined his forces.

The situation in Italy, however, was much more serious, and Sulla knew he would have to return to Italy quickly and in force. This was the context in which this aureus was struck, undoubtedly from gold surrendered by Mithradates as part of the peace settlement.

The obverse of this coin depicts a head of Venus facing right; to the right is her son, Cupid, holding a palm branch. Below is the inscription L. SVLLA. The reverse depicts two trophies, representing Sulla's battle victories over Mithradates, with the symbols of a prestigious priesthood, a jug and curved staff, between them. Although Sulla seems not to have been officially vested with this priesthood until a year or two after this coin was struck, he may have already been claiming the office, or claiming religious sanction for prolonging his command beyond its official termination. The latter is suggested by the inscription IMPER ITERVM ("General, Two Times"). These aurei were not struck in large quantities, and are very rare today, but the types were repeated on a large issue of silver denarii, which is still scarce but obtainable.

Sulla returned to Italy, seized power, made himself dictator, and attempted to reform the government, but he found no support for his plans. So he simply retired to a country estate, married a beautiful woman, and abandoned politics. He forecast that as soon as he was gone, the Roman Republic would fall back into strife and civil wars. He was right.

650 B.C.　　450　　250　　50　50　　250　　450　　650　　850　　1050　　1250　　1450 A.D.

CLEOPATRA VII ASCALON MINT TETRADRACHM

EGYPT · 50–49 B.C.

Actual size approx. 26 mm

I know of only one appearance of this coin in modern times. This was at the 1984 Christie's sale "Property of a Lady," where the tetradrachm sold for £65,000, which at the time was $80,500. Today that coin would bring at least $250,000.

Here we look upon Cleopatra, the famous Cleopatra who was the last of the Ptolemaic rulers of Egypt, and who bore a son to Julius Caesar and three children to Mark Antony. Her appearance is not what one might expect; by modern standards, she is no beauty. Her fame in the ancient world, however, did not derive from her looks; Cleopatra was famous because she competed equally with men in a male-dominated world. In a time when few women were educated, Cleopatra read, wrote, and spoke several languages. Amazingly, she was the first of her dynasty to bother to learn Egyptian, the native language of the land her family had ruled for centuries. She was also an author and was reputed to have been a chemist, experimenting with medicines and perfumes. A shrewd and ruthless politician, she survived dynastic struggles and won the affection and loyalty of two of Rome's most powerful men. Julius Caesar and Mark Antony saw in Cleopatra something much rarer in their time than beauty—a strong, educated, self-determined woman. Though slightly disreputable, to them she was irresistible.

On the silver tetradrachms Cleopatra issued in Egypt, she adhered to the common practice of putting the portrait of Ptolemy I on the obverse. This type had been endlessly repeated since the beginning of the dynasty centuries earlier. On the coins struck in Ascalon in Judea, however, we see a true portrait of the famous queen. This is the only silver coin minted by Egypt upon which she placed her image. Her portrait also appears on a Roman denarius along with Mark Antony, on Egyptian 80- and 40-drachma bronze coins, and a number of local bronze issues of cities outside Egypt but under Ptolemaic control.

This is the only silver coin minted by Egypt upon which Cleopatra placed her image.

On the reverse there is an eagle standing on a thunderbolt, emblematic of Zeus. The eagle has a palm branch over his shoulder, a symbol of victory. The legend reads, in Greek, "Queen Cleopatra." A date and various mint officials' monograms and letters appear in the field.

Only five of these portrait tetradrachms of Ascalon have been recorded.

CAESAR PORTRAIT DENARIUS

ROME · 44 B.C.

Actual size approx. 19 mm

In the 1970s a Julius Caesar portrait denarius would cost $500, in the 1980s $2,500, with some reaching $5,000. Today an average coin is $3,500 to $6,000, and an exceptional one with a good strike and centering as much as $20,000. These coins frequently are found worn, off-center, and struck with flattened dies, which results in a weak image.

Julius Caesar conquered Gaul for Rome in a series of campaigns lasting 10 years. In 49 B.C., when his enemies threatened to deprive him of his army and his command, he crossed the Rubicon River and marched on Rome. By 45 B.C., after a series of battles in Spain, northern Greece, and Africa, Caesar had defeated the forces of Pompey the Great and the senatorial party, making himself master of the Roman world.

From a Senate suitably cowed and amply supplemented with his own adherents, Caesar now accepted many extraordinary, regal, and superhuman honors. These doubtless offended traditional Romans and were later viewed as having justified Caesar's assassination. One of these honors was the right to place his portrait on coinage, like the kings of the Greek East. Caesar was the first living Roman to be allowed this honor, which began a series of imperial portraits on Roman coins lasting until the fall of Constantinople in 1453.

Accordingly, the four moneyers of 44 B.C. all placed Caesar's portrait on their denarii. He is shown wearing an elaborate untied wreath, quite different from the tied laurel wreaths that later crowned most emperors on their coins. It might represent the golden wreaths traditionally worn by victorious generals when they were allowed to celebrate a triumph at Rome.

Our denarius, of the moneyer M. Mettius, seems to be the earliest portrait denarius of 44 B.C. and is therefore the first Roman coin to show the portrait of a living person. Caesar's title "dictator for the fourth time"—CAESAR DICT QVART—guarantees a date before mid-February 44 B.C., for we know that by that date Caesar had accepted the title "perpetual dictator," a title that indeed appears on many of his other portrait denarii of that year. The fine style of Caesar's portrait on this denarius of Mettius confirms the type's early date.

This is one of the rarer portrait denarii of Caesar.

The lituus behind Caesar's portrait refers to his membership in the priestly college of augurs. The reverse, still in the republican spirit, refers not to Caesar but to the presumed hometown of the moneyer, Lanuvium, where the goddess Juno Sospita was particularly revered.

This is one of the rarer portrait denarii of Caesar. A. Alföldi, in his 1974 study of the denarii of 44 B.C., lists only 37 specimens of this denarius, coming from eight obverse and eight reverse dies.

650 B.C.   450   250   50   50   250   450   650   850   1050   1250   1450 A.D.

SULLA'S DREAM DENARIUS

ROME · 44 B.C.

Actual size approx. 19 mm

In Basel, Switzerland, in 1959 an example brought SFr 230.
In June 1979 in the same city, the price was SFr 4,200, and in
Zurich in 2002 an example brought SFr 8,000. Today an
Extremely Fine well-struck example would cost $10,000 or more.

Lucius Cornelius Sulla Felix, better known simply as Sulla, was in power in Rome from 97 to 80 B.C., on and off, but ruled as dictator from 82 to 80 B.C. He was fond of good food and the company of actors and dancers. After the deaths of his stepmother and his mistress, Nicopolis, he was wealthy enough to go into politics, and he did. After being elected quaestor he went on a campaign of conquest in Africa and Germany with his future blood rival, Gaius Marius. In 88 B.C. Sulla became consul with Quintus Pompeius Rufus, but through a series of events orchestrated by Marius, Sulla had to flee for his life—though he did so with his army. After defeating Mithradates VI of Pontus, who was overrunning Roman territories, he returned to Rome in 83 B.C. to seize power. With the help of Marcus Licinius Crassus and Pompey, among others, Sulla took Rome and became the first dictator in 120 years.

The denarius titled "Sulla's Dream" was struck in 44 B.C., not by Sulla but by moneyer Lucius Aemilius Buca, a distant relative of Sulla and a partisan of Caesar. This was the year of Julius Caesar's assassination, but the coin was struck during Caesar's lifetime; otherwise it would not have been relevant. The coin refers to both Sulla and Caesar at the same time. The Venus on the obverse is a reference to both men, as they used it on the obverses of their coinage. The reverse depicts a reclining Sulla leaning against a rock; Luna is descending from a mountain and holding a torch,

while Victory fills the background, facing Sulla with wings spread and a staff held aloft. The dream urges Sulla to strike his enemy Marius in Rome in 88 B.C. The depiction of Sulla also works as an analogy to Caesar's victory over Pompey.

These coins are beautifully designed, especially the reverse, but are very scarce. They are also very poorly executed, the reverse often poorly centered and weakly and unevenly struck.

> These coins are beautifully designed, but are very poorly executed.

Although the traditional description of the reverse of this coin as "Sulla's Dream" is still generally accepted, some scholars prefer to see it as a depiction of the myth of Selene and Endymion. This is also plausible, as Caesar and Sulla are not natural counterparts: Caesar was the nephew of Marius and narrowly escaped being killed in Sulla's proscriptions. As aedile, Caesar restored the statue of Marius to the Forum. The association of Caesar and Sulla would have been an act of supreme political cynicism. Uncertainty like this is part of the endless fascination of ancient numismatics!

650 B.C.   450   250   50   50   250   450   650   850   1050   1250   1450 A.D.

OCTAVIAN AND JULIUS CAESAR AUREUS

ROME · 43 B.C.

Actual size approx. 20 mm

In 1960 an example brought SFr 1,450; in 1975 the price was SFr 8,500; and by 1996 a coin at Sotheby's went for £15,400 (about $25,000), although they had been selling for $20,000. More recently the price jumped to $40,000, and now it is at $65,000, but a great specimen, which goes against type, would break $100,000. These aurei are usually poorly struck and somewhat ugly.

Gaius Julius Caesar Octavianus ascended to the Roman throne following the assassination of his great-uncle Julius Caesar in 44 B.C. The obverse legend of this aureus, C CAESAR COS PONT AVG, names Octavian as consul, pontifex, and augur, but it does not mention his later position of triumvir. This information tells us that the coin must have been struck between August 19, 43 B.C. (when Octavian forced the Senate to proclaim him consul—the highest office of the Roman Republic) and early November of the same year, when he formed the Second Triumvirate with Mark Antony and Lepidus.

This specimen is the only approximately contemporary aureus to show both a faithful portrait of Caesar and his lifetime titles.

The reverse shows Julius Caesar wearing the same wreath, without ties, as in the denarius portraits struck during his life-time (see No. 14, page 75) and with the titles he bore at his death: C CAESAR DICT PERP PONT MAX ("Perpetual Dictator and

Chief Pontiff"). There is no mention of deification because the triumvirs had not yet elevated him to that level. By 38 B.C., how-ever, they had done so, and Octavian had begun to call himself DIVI FILIVS ("Son of a God").

Any collector of the Twelve Caesars in gold will want a spec-imen of this aureus because it is the only approximately contem-porary aureus to show both a faithful portrait of Caesar and his lifetime titles. It is also relatively common compared to other republican or imperatorial aurei. In 1923, famed collector and numismatist Max von Bahrfeldt listed 35 of these pieces held in museums and private collections. Collectors seeking a realistic portrait of Caesar in gold can also turn to the aurei restored by Trajan, with obverses bearing either the legend C IVLIVS CAES IMP COS III ("Julius Caesar, Imperator and Consul Three Times") or DIVVS IVLIVS ("The Divine Julius"). These coins, however, are extremely rare, with fewer than 10 recorded.

Octavian, who would later change his name to Augustus, was to strike two more portrait aurei of Julius Caesar, the first in his M AGRIPPA COS DESIG ("Marcus Agrippa, Consul Desig-nate") issue of 38 B.C. and the second on a moneyer's aureus commemorating the Saecular Games of 17 B.C. Both of these aurei show rejuvenated portraits of Caesar and omit his name and titles.

BRUTUS "EID MAR" DENARIUS

ROME · 42 B.C.

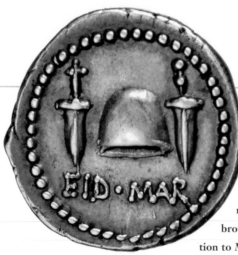

Actual size approx. 18 mm

In the Hess-Leu sale of 1958 an Extremely Fine denarius made only SFr 2,900. By 1973 the price had reached SFr 39,000, and in New York in 1985 on the night the Chicago Bears lost to Miami one failed to sell at $25,000. In the late 1990s they had risen dramatically, to $100,000 and up. In the early 2000s a museum purchased one at $164,000, and in 2007 one specimen brought $280,000. These coins range from worn barely Fine condition to Mint State, with some being copper-core denarii known as fourrées.

Brutus considered his assassination of Julius Caesar on the Ides of March, 44 B.C., to be an act of patriotism. Just as his ancestor Brutus was said to have expelled the Tarquin kings from Rome, established the Roman Republic, and become the first consul in 509 B.C., so Brutus in 44 B.C. thought that by murdering Caesar he would free the Roman people from the rule of a tyrant. According to Plutarch, Brutus told his fellow conspirator Cassius on the eve of the first battle of Philippi in 42 B.C., "On the Ides of March I devoted my life to my country, and since then I have lived in liberty and glory."

> Brutus's Eid Mar denarii are highly desirable because of their reverse commemorating Caesar's assassination.

The reverse type of our denarius, probably struck in Greece to pay Brutus's army shortly before the same battle, makes just the same statement: daggers produced liberty for Rome (symbolized by a liberty cap) on the date named in the legend, EID MAR. It was a bold and noteworthy design, so much so that it is even mentioned by an ancient historian. Dio Cassius reports that Brutus "struck coins on which were represented a liberty cap and two daggers, to show by this design and also by the inscription that he had, in concert with Cassius, given liberty to his country."

It is ironic that the obverse of the same coin nevertheless shows Brutus's portrait, with the legend BRVT IMP L PLAET CEST! Caesar, a mere two years earlier, had been the first Roman to place his own portrait on Roman coins, and that was just the sort of monarchical innovation for which he had been assassinated. L. Plaetorius Cestianus, who struck and placed his name on this and several other coins of Brutus, must have been a magistrate or officer serving under him, but is otherwise unknown.

Brutus's Eid Mar denarii are highly desirable because of their reverse commemorating Caesar's assassination, their obverse portraying the chief assassin, and their substantial rarity. In a corpus of the issue published in 1989, H.A. Cahn listed 56 denarii and also two aurei of the type, from 8 obverse and 26 reverse dies. Today the population is about 80, but many more than 80 people want one of these coins and can afford the $100,000-plus price tag.

650 B.C.   450   250   50 | 50   250   450   650   850   1050   1250   1450 A.D.

Ranked first among all ancient coins, the Brutus Eid Mar denarius offers a unique window into a famous historical event: the assassination of Julius Caesar.

Actual size approx. 20 mm

Only four of these magnificent coins exist. In 1970 one sold for SFr 75,000; in 1989 the price was SFr 270,000, and one was sold privately for over $300,000. The next time one comes to market it will once again set records if the conditions are the same as they are today.

Quintus Labienus was the son of Titus Labienus, who was perhaps Julius Caesar's most able general until shortly before the outbreak of civil war, when he joined with Pompey—and most of the Senate—to desert Caesar and flee to Epirus. The elder Labienus was killed at the Battle of Munda in 45 B.C. In 43 B.C., the year after the murder of Caesar, Quintus Labienus joined the forces of Brutus and Cassius and traveled to Parthia in hopes of gaining the assistance of that kingdom in the struggle against Antony and Octavian. After the defeat of the republicans at Philippi in 42, Labienus remained at the Parthian court, out of reach of Antony's forces, and continued to negotiate for aid. His entreaties finally bore fruit, and early in 40 B.C. Labienus and Pacorus, son of the Parthian king Orodes, led a large army into Roman Syria, where they persuaded Roman garrisons to ally with them. The Parthians and the turncoat Romans enjoyed considerable initial success, defeating Mark Antony's governor, L. Decidius Saxa, and overrunning much of Syria and Asia Minor. Their success lasted until 39 B.C., when they were decisively defeated by Antony's general Publius Ventidius in a battle in the Taurus Mountains. Labienus was subsequently beheaded, and a year later Pacorus was killed in an attack on a Roman camp.

The aureus bears the portrait of Labienus and the legend Q LABIENVS PARTHICVS IMP (Imperator) on the obverse. The reverse has no legend, but shows a standing Parthian cavalry horse, saddled and bearing a bow case. The gold and silver issues were struck from the same obverse dies; different dies were used for the gold reverses.

Most of Labienus's coinage was melted down after his death.

Rome and Parthia being sworn enemies, anything bearing the term "Parthicus" was extremely offensive to Romans. For this reason, most of Labienus's coinage was melted down after his death. About 40 denarii are recorded, but only four aurei are known. Two are in museums (London and Paris) and two are held by private collectors.

Actual size approx. 20 mm

In 1935 at the Prince Waldeck sale the price for one of these aurei was SFr 1,600; in 1975 one brought SFr 14,500, and in the Hunt mini-boom of 1980 one made SFr 92,000. In 1990 at Bank Leu the same coin brought SFr 150,000. Currently the price is in the $100,000 area.

Julius Caesar's last substantial opponent in his rise to dominance in Rome was Pompey the Great. Caesar defeated Pompey in a civil war, and Pompey fled to Egypt, where he was assassinated. But Pompey the Great left behind two sons, Sextus and Gnaeus Pompey, who continued to fight against Julius Caesar in Africa and then in Spain. Within weeks of their defeat by Caesar at Munda in 45 B.C., Gnaeus was captured and executed. Sextus escaped, raised a new army and fleet, and eventually established himself in Sicily, where his party was strengthened by men fleeing from the proscriptions of the triumvirs, the three men who headed Julius Caesar's faction after his assassination.

In April of 43 B.C., the Senate came to an arrangement with Sextus Pompey, and appointed him their naval commander with a title that Pompey the Great had also held, "Prefect of the Fleet and the Seashore." Octavian, one of the triumvirs and Caesar's nephew and adopted son, soon forced the Senate to cancel this agreement, but Sextus continued to claim the title. At this point, Sextus Pompey issued this fine aureus.

The obverse shows the head of Sextus Pompey facing right, bearded, within an oak wreath. The oak wreath was traditionally granted to those who saved the life of a fellow citizen, and here it

apparently refers to Sextus's salvation of those proscribed by the triumvirs by offering them refuge in Sicily. On the obverse, Sextus assumes his father's epithet, Magnus ("the Great"), and calls himself pious, implying that he will fulfill his obligations to avenge his family. The reverse depicts the facing busts of his father, Pompey the Great, and his brother, Gnaeus Pompey. The symbols behind their heads indicate priesthoods they held. The reverse legend gives his title as "Prefect of the Fleet and the Seashore" and indicates, EX SC, that it had been granted to him by the Senate.

For a while, Sextus Pompey seemed to be in a strong position. From his base in Sicily, he could block the grain supply to Rome, and three times he defeated fleets sent against him by Octavian, but finally Octavian and his general Agrippa defeated Sextus at Naulochus in 36 B.C. He fled to the east but was killed by a lieutenant of Mark Antony at Mitylene in 35 B.C.

Pompey the Great is portrayed on quite a few other coins, too, but this one supplies the only assured portraits of his two sons, Sextus and Gnaeus. The aureus is of considerable rarity: Jane Evans's extensive search of museums and catalogs, published in 1987, turned up only 37 specimens, from just two obverse and three reverse dies.

Actual size approx. 21 mm

This coin has always been sought after. Even in 1959 one brought SFr 360; in 1977, one brought SFr 16,000, and another that same year went for SFr 15,000. The worst of these, and they do come worn, still bring over $1,000, while the best can reach $25,000. For a decent Very Fine you should expect to pay $10,000 if Cleopatra's name is mostly there—centering is a big issue with these coins.

This coin portrays two of the most famous figures of antiquity, Mark Antony and Cleopatra. After the death of Julius Caesar, a group of his closest confidants (including his trusted right-hand man Antony, his old general Lepidus, and his nephew and adopted son Octavian) banded together to defeat his assassins. Subsequently they divided the Roman world among themselves. Lepidus, who received North Africa, soon saw the wisdom of retirement. Octavian took Italy and the western provinces, and Antony received the eastern Mediterranean. There he encountered Cleopatra, queen of Egypt—the last independent Hellenistic monarchy of significance.

The clever eastern ruler easily bent Antony to her will, making their tempestuous affair the scandal of Rome. Although Antony was married to Octavian's sister (whom he later divorced), he fathered three children by Cleopatra and later claimed that they had been married in an Egyptian ceremony. He went to war with the Parthian Empire over control of Armenia, and in 34 B.C., while celebrating his inflated claims to have conquered Armenia, gave Cleopatra the title "Queen of Kings." He also acknowledged her eldest son as the child of Julius Caesar and her three younger children as his own. Moreover, he gave lands belonging to the Roman Empire to the queen and her four children, reasoning that her ancestors had held them long before. In this context, during 34 B.C., this portrait denarius was issued at Alexandria, the capital of Egypt.

On the obverse is a portrait of Cleopatra. Below her bust is a ship's prow, symbolic of Egyptian naval power, and around is the legend CLEOPATRAE REGINAE REGVM FILIORVM REGVM ("For Cleopatra, Queen of Kings, and Her Sons Who Are Kings"). On the reverse is a portrait of Antony. Behind his head is an Armenian crown, symbolic of the war he had just concluded, and around is the Latin legend ANTONI ARMENIA DEVICTA ("Of Antony, With Armenia Conquered").

All of this played into Octavian's hands. While gathering military forces to confront Antony and Cleopatra, he publicized Antony's actions, using words designed to engender the worst possible interpretations. Antony, previously a notable general, was unable to act decisively against Octavian and was roundly defeated in a naval battle at Actium. Antony and Cleopatra retreated to Egypt, where both ultimately committed suicide as Octavian closed in. Octavian would go on to replace Rome's republican government with a monarchy, change his name to Augustus, and become the first Roman emperor.

650 B.C.   450   250   50   50   250   450   650   850   1050   1250   1450 A.D.

AUGUSTUS CISTOPHORUS WITH SPHINX REVERSE

ROME · 27 OR 26 B.C.

Actual size approx. 27 mm

In 1966 at the Niggeler sale an example brought SFr 4,000.
In Zurich in 1984 a coin of the same quality brought SFr 13,000,
and in 1989 in the same city a similar coin brought SFr 17,000.
Today the example illustrated would bring $25,000.

In the second century B.C., Pergamon, a Greek kingdom controlling what is now western Turkey, sought to control the flow of money in and out of its borders by creating the cistophorus, a silver coin based on a new weight standard, somewhat lighter than the standard tetradrachm. The cistophorus got its unusual name because the obverse type commonly bore an ivy wreath containing a cista mystica, a basket from which sacred snakes emerged. The type was associated with the god Dionysus and the mysterious, secret ceremonies honoring the god. The type persisted for more than a century, even after the area was annexed into the Roman Empire. Eventually new types were employed on these coins, but the old name remained.

The cistophorus equaled three Roman denarii, and its broad flan was the perfect backdrop for the imperial portrait and the development of the reverse type. The rarest and most distinctive of the cistophori was issued by Augustus (formerly Octavian) Caesar, the first Roman emperor, who reigned from 27 B.C. to 14 A.D. On the obverse we see a fine head of the emperor.

The reverse bears the emperor's adopted name, AVGVSTVS ("the revered one"). When he became emperor, Augustus ended a century marked by political turmoil and wars, replacing the old republican form of government with his one-man rule. As the nephew and adopted son of Julius Caesar (who had been elevated to the status of a god after his death), it seemed natural for the emperor to take such an impressive new title! In addition to his name, the reverse bears a type of particular personal significance to Augustus, a sphinx. Legends depicted the sphinx as a creature of preternatural intelligence, keeper of the most profound secrets, wise, and extremely secretive. Augustus's own signet ring was engraved with the sphinx, and historians feel that the emblem reflected his own personality. For instance, Augustus once said that he liked treason but hated traitors, and he habitually lived by the precept of keeping his friends close and his enemies closer. Late in life, he replaced his sphinx signet with a portrait of Alexander the Great. Why, of course, we do not know. Augustus was too sphinxlike to give a reason.

Although the sphinx reverse type was used on three issues of cistophori, there are only about 30 of these coins known today, struck around 27 or 26 B.C. Even rarer is an issue of gold aurei from an eastern mint, which also bears the sphinx.

Cistophori were issued by many later emperors up to Septimius Severus, frequently with portraits of fine quality and interesting reverse types. The final issue of substantial size occurred around 129 A.D., when the emperor Hadrian visited western Anatolia. At that time, many mints struck these large silver coins, generally with local deities for reverse types. A great number of these coins were struck over earlier, worn cistophori, and traces of the original type can still be seen beneath the new types.

AUGUSTUS FACING PORTRAIT DENARIUS

ROME · 17 OR 16 B.C.

Actual size approx. 20 mm

In 1934 at an Ars Classica sale, a worn example brought SFr 300, and at the 1950 H.P. Hall Collection auction a Very Fine but dinged-up example went for £21. Today the evaluation would be about $10,000. In 1979, an Extremely Fine coin with a scratch in the obverse field brought $28,000, and the same coin in 1981 fetched SFr 52,000. The coin is very rare, only a small handful appearing in the last century. An Extremely Fine coin would probably bring $75,000 today and a worn one $5,000.

Although Augustus Caesar survived until just before his 77th birthday, dying in 14 A.D., ancient sources tell us that he was frequently ill and was not expected to live long. This denarius records something that ancient historians do not: the emperor suffered a serious health crisis in 17 or 16 B.C., from which he eventually recovered.

The obverse depicts an honorary shield decorated with a facing portrait of Augustus. An inscription in tiny letters around the edge states that the shield was dedicated "By decree of the Senate, because the emperor's recuperation has guaranteed the safety of the state" (S C OB R P CVM SALVT IMP CAESAR AVGVS CONS). Two other types struck in the same year also commemorate the payment of vows for Augustus's recovery from illness. The moneyers of these coins, L. Mescinius Rufus and C. Antistius Vetus, must have served in 16 B.C., because on other coins both of them call Augustus "holder of the tribunician power for the eighth time." Ancient sources comment on the emperor's precarious health, but do not record that he fell ill precisely in 17 or 16 B.C. Similar honorary shields decorated with a facing portrait of Augustus also appeared decades later on dupondii of Tiberius, with the inscription CLEMENTIAE or MODERATIONI. Evidently the Senate voted these shields to honor the emperor's clemency and moderation.

This remarkable obverse type of Augustus is very rare, apparently occurring on only one or two obverse dies.

This remarkable obverse type of Augustus is very rare, apparently occurring on only one or two obverse dies, known from about 20 specimens. It was coupled with two reverse types. The first seems to commemorate Augustus's departure to Gaul in 16 B.C.: it shows a statue of Mars on a base that is inscribed SPQR V P / S PR S ET / RED AVG ("The Senate and the Roman people have undertaken vows for the safety of Augustus and his return [to Rome]"). The other reverse type shows a cippus that was dedicated, according to its inscription, "To Imperator Caesar Augustus, by common consent."

TIBERIUS DENARIUS
(BIBLICAL TRIBUTE PENNY)
ROMAN EMPIRE · 14–37 A.D.

Actual size approx. 19 mm

These are very common but always in demand because of their biblical significance. In the 1970s and 1980s these coins were $500 to $700 for Extremely Fine, with worn examples selling at $200. Until a few years ago Mint State examples were rarely found, but today they are found more frequently, and as such sell for up to $2,000. Fine coins now bring $350.

And they sent unto him certain of the Pharisees and of the Herodians, to catch him in his words. And when they were come, they said unto him, Master, we know that thou art true, and carest for no man; for thou regardest not the person of men, but teaching the way of God in truth: Is it lawful to give tribute to Caesar or not? Shall we give, or shall we not give? But he, knowing their hypocrisy, said unto them, Why tempt ye me? Bring me a penny that I may see it. And they brought it. And he said unto them, Whose is this image and superscription? And they said unto him, Caesar's. And Jesus answering said unto them, Render to Caesar the things that are Caesar's, and to God the things that are God's. (Mark 12:13–17, with parallel passages at Matthew 22:16 and Luke 20:22)

This is the famous "tribute penny" of the Bible. Two aspects require explanation. First, "Caesar" was the family name of Julius Caesar and his nephew, Augustus Caesar, who became the first Roman emperor. "Caesar" soon became a title, as did "Augustus"; every Roman emperor was both Caesar and Augustus. The reigning Caesar at the time of Jesus' ministry was Tiberius, the adopted son of Augustus. Second, the English term "penny" is the King James Bible translation of the denomination indicated in the original Greek of the New Testament: the Roman denarius. This coin is by a large margin the most common variety of the denarius coined by Tiberius, and the most likely candidate for being the biblical tribute penny.

On the obverse we see the head of Tiberius crowned with a laurel wreath. On some examples, presumably the earliest, Tiberius is portrayed as young and smooth-faced, which is odd because he was 56 years old when he succeeded Augustus in 14 A.D. On other coins he is shown with a craggy, obviously aged face, which was probably accurate since he was 78 at the time of his death in 37 A.D. Around the portrait is a highly abbreviated

Latin legend that may be rendered in English as "Tiberius Caesar, Son of the Divine Augustus, Augustus."

The reverse depicts Livia, the wife of Augustus and mother of Tiberius, seated and holding a long scepter and an olive branch, the symbol of peace. She is flanked by the abbreviated Latin for "Chief Priest," one of Tiberius's most prestigious titles.

The question of whether it was lawful to pay money—taxes—to Caesar was intended to trap Jesus. If he had answered that money ought *not* be paid to Caesar, Jesus would have been guilty of treason, but if he had answered that money *ought* to be paid to Caesar, he would have seemed to be submissive to the hated Romans. Jesus' answer neatly avoided both alternatives and at the same time defined the duty owed to both the secular authorities and God.

The tribute penny denarii are common, with thousands surviving, and they are very enthusiastically sought by collectors because they are the surviving objects most closely associated with Jesus. There is always the chance that this or any other tribute penny may have been the actual coin mentioned in the Bible.

650 B.C.   450   250   50   50   250   450   650   850   1050   1250   1450 A.D.

JERUSALEM TYRIAN-TYPE SHEKEL

JUDEA · 33 A.D.

Actual sizes approx. 19-24 mm

These coins were not recognized as what they are until recently. They sell for from $400 to $1,200, with those from the crucifixion year (33 A.D.) costing from $800 to $4,000.

The Jerusalem Tyrian-type shekel has been included among the 100 Greatest Ancient Coins not for its beauty—it is in fact rather crudely executed—but for its great historical appeal. This coin is of particular interest because it was struck in 33 A.D., the year of the crucifixion of Jesus.

> This coin is of particular interest because it was struck in 33 A.D., the year of the crucifixion of Jesus.

From the days of Moses each Jewish male over the age of 20 had been required to pay an annual tax of half a shekel to support first the tabernacle in the wilderness and later the temple in Jerusalem. To ensure that the offerings were of exactly the required weight of silver, the coins used for this purpose could only be those approved by temple priests. The silver shekels struck by the Phoenician city of Tyre fulfilled this role from 127/126 B.C. until 19/18 B.C., when Rome lowered the percentage of silver from close to 95% to only 80% and flooded the market with inferior coins. This created a potentially disastrous problem for the temple in Jerusalem. How were the temple offerings now to be made? The crisis was averted when, it appears, the priests decided

to set up their own mint within the temple itself and began to strike shekels of the Tyrian type.

The Jerusalem shekel differed somewhat from the earlier shekels of Tyre. The new shekels were thicker, smaller in diameter, and flatter, with the monogram KP in the right field of the reverse. Rome would not allow the Jews to replace the head of the Phoenician god Melqarth on the obverse or the eagle and lettering on the reverse. Consequently, according to Ya'akov Meshorer in *A Treasury of Jewish Coins*, "as an expression of contempt for the Tyrian designs on the shekels, the Jerusalem mint executed them with demonstrative crudity."

In place of the changing letters of the various mint officials on the Tyrian originals, the Jerusalem shekels uniformly carry a monogram that may represent the first letters of the Greek work meaning "by the authority." The shekels did continue to bear the dates, year by year, from 19/18 B.C. until the First Jewish Revolt against the Romans began in 65/66 A.D. In that year the issue of Tyrian-type shekels ended, and, more notably, the minting of the first truly Jewish silver shekels began. These new shekels, bearing the Hebrew inscriptions "Shekel of Israel" and "Holy Jerusalem," became one of the models for the modern Israeli shekels used today.

CALIGULA THREE SISTERS SESTERTIUS

ROME · 37-38 A.D.

Actual size approx. 35 mm

This coin normally comes corroded and worn, but in the desire to make worn coins look better, many of them have been recut or tooled to improve the detail that has worn away. In addition, because of the coin's wide appeal, there are many cast forgeries, which are easy to detect but still influence the market. As a result of all of this, values vary widely. Worn coins with minor tooling cost $4,500, but an untouched Extremely Fine example can exceed $60,000.

Caligula, whose real name was Gaius Julius Caesar Augustus Germanicus, was the third Roman emperor, ruling from 37 to 41 A.D. A young man when he came to the throne, Caligula was initially popular with everyone—but then things started to go wrong. Opinion was, and remains, divided as to whether the new emperor always had a streak of insanity about him, became intoxicated with his newfound power, or suddenly went mad. Another theory is that Caligula fell seriously ill shortly after becoming emperor, supposedly accidentally poisoned by a love potion—and today we know that one popular Roman love potion of the time can cause toxic insanity. Whatever the cause, Caligula soon proved to be wildly eccentric, hedonistic, cruel, and arbitrary. His behavior became so odd that no story about him seemed impossible, and, unfortunately for modern historians, unreliable anecdotes multiplied greatly.

Some of the most scandalous stories claimed that Caligula had unnatural relations with his three sisters. In fact, he certainly granted them unusual honors at the beginning of his reign. They were allowed the same privileges as the highly honored Roman priestesses known as the Vestal Virgins, seats in the imperial box at the Circus, and the inclusion of their names in annual state vows and oaths of allegiance. Moreover, the three sisters appear on an extraordinary bronze sestertius. The obverse portrays Caligula, surrounded by his name and titles. On the reverse we see his sisters, gracefully depicted, along with their names: Agrippina,

Drusilla, and Iulia. The initials S C (for "Senatus Consulto"), standard on Roman bronze coins of the first three centuries A.D., indicate that the Senate approved the issue.

This state of affairs did not endure for long. Drusilla died in June 38, and Agrippina and Julia were banished in 39 because of supposed involvement in a plot against Caligula. The type depicting the three sisters was discontinued at Drusilla's death.

Caligula was initially popular with everyone —but then things started to go wrong.

Caligula's behavior grew increasingly strange and dangerous to those around him, though we need not credit *all* the stories—many very strange indeed—that are told about this ruler (many by the gossip-mongering historian Suetonius). Whatever the true extent of his bizarre behavior, Caligula grew so dangerous that a palace conspiracy led to his assassination in 41, ending his short and troubled reign.

There are at least a hundred examples of the Three Sisters sestertius known. Demand is much greater than the available quantity because of the notoriety of the emperor and the stories about his sisters.

BRITANNICUS SESTERTIUS

Actual size approx. 35 mm

Before the former communist countries of Eastern Europe opened up, these sestertii were among the great rarities of the Roman series. In the 19th century, Henry Cohen gave them the stratospheric value of 2,500 French gold francs. In the 1960s the Mazzini coin sold for $30,000. Now there are a good number of low-grade Britannicus sestertii available at $5,000 to $15,000, but great examples like the one sold in Gemini I in 2005 still bring $70,000.

Britannicus, the son of the Roman emperor Claudius I and the empress Messalina, was born in 41 A.D., the first year of Claudius's reign. Claudius was given the title Britannicus a few years later, when the Senate bestowed it upon him (and his descendants) after his conquest of Britain in 43. In 48, Claudius executed Messalina and her lover for plotting to take over the empire and then married his own niece, Agrippina II. In 51, Claudius adopted Agrippina's son, Nero, who was four years older than Britannicus. When Claudius died in 54, Nero alone was proclaimed emperor. Four months later Britannicus suddenly died, stricken at dinner.

The sestertius of Britannicus is one of the key coins of the entire Roman series.

Nero proved to be a terrible emperor, both scandalizing and terrifying the conservative senators in Rome. After his death in 68, Roman historians, almost all of whom were senators or friends and allies of senators, were eager to blacken his reputation as much as possible. Nero was accused of every possible crime, both real and imaginary, including poisoning Britannicus.

The accusation may be false. Nero was already securely on the throne, and there is no indication of any active plot to replace him with Britannicus, who was still a child. Moreover, Britannicus suffered from severe epilepsy and the description of his death is consistent with a massive epileptic seizure. Titus, a childhood friend of Britannicus, was present at the dinner at which he died.

There were no coins struck for Britannicus at the imperial mints at Rome and Lugdunum. The coinage of 51 to 54 from these mints shows only Claudius, Agrippina II, and Nero. A smaller mint in Thrace, however, struck sestertii portraying Britannicus. The obverse shows the bust of young Britannicus surrounded by his formal name, TI CLAVDIVS CAESAR AVG F BRITANNICVS, "Tiberius Claudius Caesar Britannicus son of the Augustus [emperor]." The reverse depicts the striding figure of Mars, the god of war, holding spear and shield. On either side of Mars are the initials S C, which typically appear on Roman imperial bronze coins to indicate they were issued with the authorization of the Senate.

The sestertius of Britannicus is one of the key coins of the entire Roman series. Until recently, only about a dozen specimens, mainly in mediocre condition, were recorded. However, when ancient coins began emerging from Eastern Europe after the fall of the iron curtain in 1989, the number of available specimens rose considerably. There are now more than 30 known.

650 B.C.   450   250   50   50   250   450   650   850   1050   1250   1450 A.D.

Actual size approx. 32 mm

These coins are only scarce, but also immensely popular; thus, the high prices are relative to their rarity. In the 1970s the prices were at $12,000 to $15,000. The coin illustrated here would probably bring $60,000 or more.

In 42 A.D., because silting was endangering shipping in Rome's original harbor at the mouth of the Tiber, Claudius I began building a new harbor some two miles north that would be linked with the Tiber—and thus to Rome—by canal. The work was completed during the reign of Claudius's successor, the infamous emperor Nero. This sestertius was struck at Rome circa 64 to 65 A.D. in celebration of the accomplishment.

While the obverse of the coin shows a handsome portrait of Nero surrounded by his name and titles, the reverse is far more interesting. Here the coin gives us a bird's-eye view of the new port and the activity that took place there every day. Neptune reclines at the bottom of the scene between two curving piers, or moles, that enclose the harbor. Warehouses and a temple have been built on the left mole, while the right mole serves as a breakwater. On the left mole, a man sacrifices at an altar, presumably thanking the gods for a safe arrival or entreating their protection for an upcoming journey. Another man appears to be sitting on a rock at the end of the right mole. A lighthouse surmounted by a statue of the emperor rises from an island at the mouth of the harbor. (The surviving remains, though, indicate that the lighthouse actually stood at the end of the left mole.)

Four ships are depicted in successive port activities, illustrating a typical freighter's use of the harbor. At the top left, one ship enters the harbor under full sail. A second ship lies at anchor in the center of the harbor while men on deck or climbing in the rigging take in her sails. Another ship is moored on the left pier while her cargo is unloaded. One man works on deck and another crosses the gangplank to shore. Finally, to the right of the lighthouse, a fourth ship is being rowed out of the harbor. Several other vessels fill out the scene.

> While the obverse of the coin shows a handsome portrait of Nero, the reverse is far more interesting.

The Port of Ostia type was introduced on sestertii of Rome in 64 to 65 A.D., and was copied on sestertii of Lugdunum from 64 to 68. Occurring in dozens of different varieties, this coin is not a great rarity, but is eagerly sought because of the novelty and intricacy of its depiction.

Actual size approx. 19 mm

In 1962, a denarius brought SFr 12,500; in 1974 the price was SFr 48,000, and in the spring of that year at Numismatic Ars Classica a coin in Extremely Fine condition brought $90,000.

By 68 A.D., Nero had become thoroughly unpopular with many Romans. He was self-indulgent, tyrannical, and inept. The first of several revolts—led by a disaffected Gaul named Vindex—broke out in 68, but was soon suppressed. Galba, a governor in Spain, was next to raise the flag of revolution. As Nero's soldiers defected, Galba moved toward Italy. After Nero committed suicide, the Senate recognized Galba as emperor, but his problems also persisted. In North Africa the governor L. Clodius Macer had also revolted and by April 68 ceased to support Galba, hoping instead to promote his own ambitions.

Fewer than 20 of these portrait coins survive.

Clodius Macer presented himself as a man devoted to the ideals of the old republic as it had existed more than a century earlier, before the emperors had taken power. He placed his name and portrait on some of his coins, but he appears bareheaded, like an old republican senator, without the imperial laurel wreath. He even put the initials S C on the obverse of his coin, indicating (falsely) that the coins had been issued by senatorial decree. He placed a war galley and his official title, "Propraetor [governor] of Africa," on the reverse of his portrait coins.

Macer had only a small land army, but his naval forces were more substantial. He could hope to defend North Africa with his ships and perhaps win by intercepting the vital grain shipments from northern Africa and Egypt to Rome.

But it all came to nothing. Macer simply did not have an adequate power base. Soon he and his navy were reduced to the status of little more than pirates, and by October 68 his revolt had failed and he was dead. Fewer than 20 of his portrait coins survive.

Galba failed too, a victim of a plot that put Otho on the throne. Otho lasted only three months before Vitellius made himself emperor. Vitellius in turn was emperor for barely seven months before the vigorous general Vespasian, relying on the eastern armies, eliminated him and restored stability to Rome.

Of the six men (Nero, Galba, Macer, Otho, Vitellius, and Vespasian) who claimed the leadership of Rome in the years 68 and 69 A.D., Macer is the most mysterious. Were his evident republican sentiments just a ploy to win support, or did he really respect and hope to restore the old institutions?

650 B.C.   450   250   50   50   250   450   650   850   1050   1250   1450 A.D.

FIRST REVOLT YEAR 5 SHEKEL

JUDEA · 70 A.D.

Actual size approx. 23 mm

These coins have always had a great attraction to collectors of biblical, Christian, and Jewish coins. In 1890, a small group of these coins was found stored in the basement of a London dealer. The coins were condemned as fake then, but later were proven to the satisfaction of most people to be genuine. These coins now sell for between $40,000 and $75,000. Other coins not found in the London dealer's basement are possibly from another mint, as they are of a different and somewhat better style. They bring $125,000. There is no year 5 shekel in less than Extremely Fine condition.

In 66 A.D., after decades of misrule and cultural misunderstanding, the Jews of Judea rose up against their Roman masters. Although the revolt of tiny and poor Judea against the might of Rome was doomed from the outset, the Jews proved to be fierce warriors and the Romans suffered many losses until, aided by conflict within the Jewish ranks, they crushed the insurrection.

During the revolt, the Judeans issued coins of purely Jewish types whose designs expressed their desire for political and cultural independence. The most important of these coins, the Jewish War or First Revolt silver shekel of year 5, is a classic rarity. It is surprising that they exist at all, given that by the beginning of the fifth year, the revolt was in serious trouble. Overwhelming Roman forces were closing in from all sides, most of the countryside had already been re-conquered, and Jerusalem itself was under siege. Only a few remote outposts, such as Masada, still stood against the foreign armies. Within four months after the coin was issued, Jerusalem fell to the foe, burnt and destroyed, and all mintage of shekels ceased.

On the obverse we see a chalice, the temple vessel used for the offering of the first grain harvest, surrounded by the inscription, in archaic Hebrew script, "Shekel of Israel." Above the chalice are Hebrew letters indicating "Year 5." On the reverse is a branch

bearing three pomegranates (a traditional Jewish decoration), and around it, again in ancient Hebrew script, "Holy Jerusalem." The edges of each First Revolt shekel consist of three flattened rows all around the coin, made with a delicate hammer.

> The Judeans issued coins whose designs expressed their desire for political and cultural independence.

Shekels were minted in each of the five years of the revolt, with year 1 being scarce, years 2 and 3 the most common, year 4 very rare, and year 5 the rarest. The coinage is eloquent testimony to the struggle of a people to preserve their religion and culture, even in the face of overwhelming power. Both their dream and their coinage, however, survived even this misfortune and endure today.

Many of the 25 year 5 shekels recorded today were found on Masada.

650 B.C.   450   250   50   50   250   450   650   850   1050   1250   1450 A.D.

Actual size approx. 35 mm

Like the Port of Ostia coins, the Judea Capta coins are only scarce, but they command high prices because of their extreme popularity. They often come worn and corroded, which makes nicely patinated, well-preserved sestertii quite pricey. For the last 30 years Very Fine coins have cost $3,000 to $5,000, with exceptional sestertii reaching $20,000. Corroded or very worn coins still bring in the neighborhood of $1,000.

We have just seen a Jewish coin from the First Jewish Revolt against Rome. Here is a Roman coin issued to commemorate the same war. On the obverse is the head of the emperor Vespasian, depicted with uncompromising reality. He was a tough old soldier in advanced middle age. He wears the imperial laurel wreath, but his short-cropped military haircut and stern face show us his essential character. Around his portrait is a Latin legend filled with abbreviations, IMP CAES VESPASIAN AVG P M TR P P P COS III ("Emperor Caesar Vespasian Augustus, High Priest, Holder of the Power of Tribune, Father of His Country, Consul Three Times"). The consulship number indicates that the coin was struck in 71 A.D. The revolt had begun in 66, and Jerusalem fell in 70, but the last embers of resistance were not stamped out until 73.

The reverse is of greater interest. In the center is a palm tree, symbol of Judea. To the right sits a Jewish woman, the personification of the Jewish people, in an attitude of mourning, while to the left stands the proud general Vespasian, one foot resting on a helmet representing armor captured from the Jewish enemy. In one hand he holds a spear and in the other a parazonium, a short sword. Surrounding the scene is the simple legend IVDAEA CAPTA ("Judea Captured").

Another variety of the sestertius shows a somewhat different scene. To the left of the palm in place of Vespasian stands a Jewish captive, his arms bound, and behind him captured spears and shields.

Coins celebrating the capture of Judea were also struck in silver and in smaller bronze denominations, and not just in a single issue, but rather throughout the reign of Vespasian and that of his son Titus. Provincial coins continued to celebrate the theme even during the reign of Vespasian's second son, Domitian (emperor from 81 to 96 A.D.), who had played no role in the war.

The failed First Jewish Revolt against the Romans was an event of greatest importance. It led to the destruction of the Jewish temple in Jerusalem, which had for centuries been the center of Jewish religious life. Judaism survived but followed a new course. Henceforth it would be centered on local synagogues. The war was also important to the development of Christianity. Earliest Christianity was in essence a sect within Judaism, one of many, but Christians had largely failed to support the revolt against Rome. The resulting hostility hastened and perhaps made inevitable the split that made Christianity and Judaism two separate religions.

The war was an embarrassment for the Romans. One of their smallest and poorest provinces had revolted. Despite the might of their empire and their superb army, it took four years to capture Jerusalem and several years more to subdue the last revolutionaries. All the Romans could do was put the best possible interpretation on events. They represented the affair as a glorious victory rather than what it really was: a failure to administer their empire in an enlightened and civilized manner.

650 B.C. | 450 | 250 | 50 | 50 | 250 | 450 | 650 | 850 | 1050 | 1250 | 1450 A.D.

Actual size approx. 35 mm

Wanted by all, including the Romans themselves, these coins come in very worn condition. This is probably because the sports-crazy Romans must have carried them as pocket pieces. Coins in only Very Good to Fine bring $15,000 to $20,000 and have for many years. The best specimen to come up in many years is the Hunt coin sold by Sotheby's in 1990 for $79,750. That coin would bring double that amount today.

After the turbulent "Year of the Four Emperors," Vespasian became emperor of Rome. Seeking ways to secure his position, he hit upon the scheme of building an immense sports center for the capital. The location of the new building, the site of Nero's Golden House, was picked with care. The message was clear: Vespasian would replace Nero's extravagant self-indulgence with a building for the common enjoyment of the population of Rome.

The construction of the enormous building went on throughout most of Vespasian's 10-year reign, and it was still not complete at the time of his death in 79. Vespasian was succeeded by his son Titus, who was able to dedicate the building in June of 80, although some of the work remained incomplete. Titus died prematurely in 81, and the last details of the building were finally completed under his brother, Domitian, emperor from 81 to 96.

Officially named the Amphitheatrum Flavium (Flavium was the family name of Vespasian and his sons), the structure became popularly known as the Colosseum because of its size and because it stood next to an enormous statue, or colossus, of Nero.

The Colosseum was indeed immense. It stood more than 160 feet high and could seat 50,000 people. The 80 entrances allowed spectators to enter and leave quickly and efficiently. The core of the building was constructed of concrete, clad with marble in the area of the better seats and travertine in the cheaper sections. The fourth story supported a retractable roof of canvas. The floor of the Colosseum was made of heavy wooden timbers covered with dirt. Below were cells for animals and prisoners doomed to fight in the arena.

Gladiatorial contests and animal fights were the chief amusements of the Colosseum, but early in its history the floor was sometimes removed and the lower levels flooded for naval combats. The Colosseum was dedicated with games that lasted 100 days, and celebrations of important victories were similar in scale. It is estimated that as many as 10,000 people died in the games at the Colosseum and an immensely greater number of animals. Gladiatorial combats were discontinued in 404, but animal baiting and hunts continued to be held into the sixth century.

The Colosseum sestertius occurs in two main variants, one struck during Titus's lifetime (25 of which are recorded) and the other shortly after his death (10 recorded; illustrated above). Both provide an aerial perspective of the immense building, flanked by a monumental fountain, the Meta Sudans, on the left, and by a portico of the Baths of Titus on the right. The outer wall of the Colosseum rises four stories, with empty arches on the first story, arches filled with statues on the second and third stories, and rectangular compartments containing globes and squares on the fourth story. Within we see tiers of spectators, and a central arch probably representing the imperial box. The reverse shows Titus as the bringer of peace after victory: wearing a toga and holding a branch and roll, he sits left on a curule chair. The curule legs encompass a globe symbolizing the universe, while captured weapons are scattered on all sides.

TRAJAN DANUBE BRIDGE SESTERTIUS

ROME · 103–111 A.D.

Actual size approx. 35 mm

These coins are only scarce but normally come in worn condition, in which state they are worth $250 to $1,000. Extremely Fine examples are very rare, and the one illustrated here is worth $15,000.

The obverse of this bronze sestertius depicts the emperor Trajan surrounded by his name and titles. Trajan was an able general who ruled from 98 to 117 A.D. During the first part of his reign he fought a long and difficult series of wars against the Dacians, a northern people who lived mainly in the area of modern Romania, which Trajan annexed to the Roman Empire.

The reverse of the sestertius depicts one of Trajan's greatest architectural achievements, one that was associated with the long and difficult war that led to the defeat and annexation of Dacia: a magnificent bridge that spanned the mighty Danube River. In reality, the bridge was much bigger than could be depicted on the coin. It consisted of huge timber foundations driven into the river bottom and surmounted by 20 massive stone piers, which were topped with wooden arches that, in turn, supported a road. In addition, monumental ornamented stone entrance gates stood at each end. The coin type abbreviates the bridge to the two entrance gates and only one arch.

The bridge was celebrated throughout the ancient world as an architectural marvel, but its underlying message was still greater: nothing stood in the way of the Roman Empire. Not even great natural barriers, such as the Danube River, could protect the barbarian who earned the wrath of the most powerful empire in the world. The bridge was more than an engineering achievement,

more than a militarily useful roadway—it was a propaganda statement about the strength and reach of the Roman Empire. The reverse legend has propaganda value as well: S P Q R OPTIMO PRINCIPI ("To the Senate and People of Rome the Best Emperor"). Additionally, the letters S C, common on bronze coinage, indicate that the coin was issued with the approval of the Senate. It seems appropriate that the Roman Empire reached its greatest size during Trajan's reign.

> The reverse of the sestertius depicts one of Trajan's greatest architectural achievements.

The Danube bridge sestertii are not rare, but they are difficult to find in Extremely Fine condition and are very popular with collectors. The smaller dupondii and *asses*, respectively one half and one quarter of the value of the sestertius, are perhaps a little scarcer. Their smaller flans offer less space for detail in depictions of the bridge, but they are still prized by collectors.

HADRIAN YEAR 874 OF ROME AUREUS

ROME · 121 A.D.

Actual size approx. 20 mm

In 1973, at a Bank Leu sale, an Extremely Fine example brought SFr 42,000, which is a good escalation from the 1967 price of SFr 3,200 in the Niggeler sale. In the 2000s a Very Fine sold for $25,000.

O n April 21, 121 A.D., the emperor Hadrian instituted chariot races to commemorate the day on which the city of Rome had been founded. For the rest of Roman history, the commemoration of Rome's birthday on April 21 would be a major holiday throughout the entire empire. To make the day even more significant, it was almost certainly then that Hadrian also dedicated his immense temple of Roma and Venus that took nearly the rest of his reign to complete. The foundations of the temple still survive today, though most of the building has long since been cannibalized to build other structures.

The reverse type is unique in all of Roman coinage.

In Hadrian's time, Christianity was still a despised minority religion in the Roman Empire. Moreover, even Christians were not yet measuring time in relation to the birth of Jesus, so naturally the year was not known to the Romans as 121 A.D. For them it was 874, the number of years since the founding of Rome in what we know as 753 B.C.

No record of Hadrian's establishment of new games to commemorate the founding of Rome exists anywhere in surviving

Roman literature. It is known only because of a rare issue of gold coins, aurei, of which only about 15 specimens have been discovered. That these coins were a special issue is made evident on the obverse, where the inscription IMP CAES HADRIANVS AVG COS III ("Emperor Caesar Hadrian Augustus, Three Times Consul") has been substituted for the usual IMP CAESAR TRAIAN HADRIANVS AVG ("Emperor Caesar Trajan Hadrian Augustus"). In addition, the portrait of Hadrian is unusually finely executed.

The reverse type is unique in all of Roman coinage. It depicts a reclining genius (guiding spirit) of the Circus with his body facing left but his head facing right. He is shown balancing a chariot wheel on his knee with his right hand, while his left arm is wrapped around the turning posts of the Circus. Even more striking is the reverse legend, which reads: ANN DCCCLXXIIII NAT VRB P CIR CON ("Year 874 Since the Birth of the City; First Circus Games Established"). The inscription is unusual because Roman coins were not normally dated in the conventional sense. Historians have often been able to determine when a coin had been struck because the number of times an emperor held specific titles and offices was usually recorded on imperial coins. The only other Roman imperial coin known to bear a specific date is one commissioned by the usurper emperor Pacatian in 248 A.D., commemorating the year 1001 of Rome.

650 B.C.   450   250   50   50   250   450   650   850   1050   1250   1450 A.D.

BAR KOCHBA
YEAR 1 TETRADRACHM

JUDEA · 132 A.D.

Actual size approx. 27 mm

Almost all of the Jewish war coins were much rarer before Israel won the 1967 war. After that, a flood of Jewish coins for both wars with the Romans came to market, but not the year 1 variety, which remains rare. In 1968, at a Hess-Leu sale, the price was SFr 15,500; in 1980, it was $30,000, and in 1981 it was SFr 46,000. Today one of these coins would be worth $65,000. These coins only come in Extremely Fine or better, though there are normally areas of flatness since they were all overstruck on earlier Roman coins.

In 132 A.D., the Second Jewish Revolt against Rome broke out, provoked by the Roman declaration of Jerusalem as a purely Roman city to be renamed Alea Capitolina and the construction of a temple to Jupiter on the ruins of a Jewish temple. Led by Shimon Bar Kochba, this uprising was an even more desperate affair than the first, lasting until 135 A.D. Judea had never completely recovered from the devastation of the first revolt, and Bar Kochba never gained control of Jerusalem. Still, the revolt lasted through four years of heavy fighting and tremendous bloodshed. To subdue the revolt, the Romans brought their finest general all the way from Britain and transferred many troops from as far away as the western European provinces.

The coins of Bar Kochba proclaim the religious, political, and cultural ideals of the revolutionaries.

The coins of Bar Kochba, especially the silver tetradrachm of the first year, proclaim the religious, political, and cultural ideals of the revolutionaries. The obverse shows the facade of the temple at Jerusalem, which had actually been destroyed at the end of the

first revolt. Within the door of the temple can be glimpsed the Ark of the Covenant. Circling the obverse, in archaic Hebrew script, is the inscription "Jerusalem." On the reverse is a group of four species of plants associated with the Tabernacles Festival and the inscription in the same archaic script: "Year One of the Redemption of Israel."

Tetradrachms of the second year of the revolt changed the reverse legend to "Year Two of the Freedom of Israel." During the third and fourth years inscriptions read simply, "For the Freedom of Jerusalem." The message seems to evolve from religious hope for redemption to the political hope of freedom.

These coins are always struck over the silver tetradrachms issued by the Roman emperors in Syria. Because the Jews never held Jerusalem, they did not have the ability to make planchets; thus, overstriking became a necessity. There is something symbolic in the overstriking of the hated images of the Roman emperors with messages of redemption and freedom. Hopes of freedom were not realized during this revolt, but they lived on. Many tetradrachms and drachms were minted by the Jews during the revolt, as well as bronze coins, but the year 1 tetradrachm is the rarest and most beautiful.

Actual size approx. 35 mm

These bronze coins circulated for many decades and almost always come in very worn condition, although they are still much sought after. Expect to pay in the range of $1,000 for average Very Good coins to $10,000 for Extremely Fine or nearly so.

Control of Egypt was essential to the success of any Roman emperor. Egyptian grain sustained Rome for three months of the year, and high taxes extracted from Egypt filled the imperial coffers. Egypt was ruled by officials appointed personally by the emperor. In order to control the flow of wealth in and out of the land, only one currency—struck under imperial supervision at the chief city, Alexandria—circulated in Egypt. The largest and most outstanding of the coins made especially for Egypt were the bronze drachms. The most impressive of the Alexandrian drachms occur in the series struck during the reign of Antoninus Pius (138–161 A.D.).

According to mythology, Hercules, driven mad by the hostility of the goddess Hera, slew his wife and children. To expiate his crime, Hercules subjected himself to his evil uncle, Eurystheus, for 12 years. Hercules was commanded by his uncle to complete 10 tasks, all virtually suicide missions. Eurystheus disallowed two of Hercules' tasks on technicalities, so the hero had to perform a dozen tasks before he could leave his uncle's service: killing the lion of Nemea; killing the hydra of Lerna; capturing the Ceryneian hind; capturing the boar of Mount Erymanthus; cleaning the stables of Augeas; killing the Stymphalian birds; capturing the Cretan bull; capturing the man-eating mares of Diomedes; retrieving the belt of Hippolyta, queen of the Amazons; taking the cattle of Geryon; retrieving the golden apples of the Hesperides; and bringing Cerberus, the three-headed hound that guarded the Underworld, back to the land of the living.

Each of these labors is represented on the bronze drachms issued under Pius. Thus, on the "Apples of Hesperides" type (below), Hercules is depicted with his trademark club and lion skin advancing to pick the apples from a tree around which lies coiled the slain serpent Ladon, guardian of the tree. On the "Boar of Mount Erymanthus" type (above), the mighty Hercules carries the fierce boar on his shoulder to present it as ordered to Eurystheus. The panicked, cowardly Eurystheus hides in a large wine jar.

The Alexandria bronze drachms of Antoninus Pius were usually struck from well-made dies and bear an excellent, detailed portrait of the emperor on the obverse. Special care seems to have been lavished on the Labors of Hercules series, and these coins are especially handsome. Collectors eagerly seek them, and they are scarce in any condition. When they are encountered, they are frequently in very worn condition. Well-preserved specimens are as rare as they are handsome.

COMMODUS PORTRAIT SESTERTIUS WITH LION SKIN OF HERCULES

ROME · CIRCA 191 A.D.

Actual size approx. 20 mm

In 1970, a Very Fine sestertius brought SFr 800, and in 2004 another Very Fine sestertius fetched SFr 9,000 at Numismatica Ars Classica. A gold aureus recently sold for $150,000, which seems appropriate since there are only a few known.

The Age of the Good Emperors ended in 180 A.D. when Marcus Aurelius, the philosopher emperor, died and was succeeded by his unworthy son, the infamous Emperor Commodus. Commodus let himself believe all the flattery that necessarily followed an emperor, and his inflated ego led him to appear in the arena as a gladiator. Gladiators, however, occupied the bottom of the Roman social order, so the elite regarded it as particularly repugnant for an emperor to associate with such people, much less aspire to be one. Commodus's gladiatorial opponents were, of course, either carefully drugged or confined behind an iron barrier and could not possibly harm him.

Commodus also came to believe that he was the reincarnation of the mythical hero Hercules. This attempt to identify himself with the demigod culminated late in 192. The occasion may have been a fire that destroyed large sections of Rome, probably in the summer of 192. This led Commodus to decide that he, in the guise of Hercules, would refound the city as his own colony, styling it the "Immortal, Fortunate Colony of the Whole Earth." The Senate voted him the title "The Roman Hercules," and statues were erected throughout the city showing Commodus wearing a lion skin and carrying a club, the traditional attributes of Hercules. The lion skin and club were carried before him when Commodus moved through the city and were placed on a gilded chair in the theater during games. A gold statue weighing 1,000 pounds was erected, showing Commodus plowing behind a team of a bull and a cow, refounding Rome. The Senate decreed that Commodus's reign should be termed the "Golden Age," and even the months of the year were renamed after him and the extravagant titles he claimed, starting each year with Amazonius and progressing through Invictus, Pius, Felix, Lucius, Aelius, Aurelius, Commodus, Augustus, Herculeus, Romanus, and finally Exsuperatorius.

In response to these events, the mint of Rome placed the head of the emperor wearing the lion skin of Hercules on the obverse of normal coins for the first time, combined with three reverse types dedicated to Commodus as the Roman Hercules. The commonest of these three types, occurring on aurei, denarii, sestertii, and *asses*, showed a club in a wreath, with the legend HERCVLI ROMANO AVGVSTO or its abbreviation.

Considerably scarcer was the type showing a club flanked by a bow and a quiver, without the wreath. This type also occurs on aurei and denarii.

The third and rarest reverse type on ordinary coins of this issue showed Commodus as Hercules, wearing a lion skin over his head and holding a club, plowing behind an ox and a cow, refounding Rome as the legend declares: HERC ROM CONDITORI. This type, which occurs on aurei, sestertii, and dupondii, may depict the thousand-pound gold statue that third-century Roman historian Dio Cassius mentions.

In addition to—or maybe because of—his extravagance, Commodus grew increasingly paranoid. He had more than a dozen senators executed on flimsy pretexts and was feared by the rest of the Senate, as well as by former friends and associates. It was all too much. A plot was hatched and on the last day of December 192, with the complicity of his imperial bodyguards, Commodus was assassinated.

650 B.C.   450   250   50   50   250   450   650   850   1050   1250   1450 A.D.

CLODIUS ALBINUS AUREUS

Actual size approx. 21 mm

In a Christie's sale of 1984, an aureus brought £48,600. At Sotheby's in 1996 the coin fetched £154,000. The Hunt coin of 1990 brought $214,500, and subsequently that coin was sold privately for over $250,000. A few low-grade specimens found in India have sold in the $15,000 area.

When Septimius Severus, the governor of Upper Pannonia, revolted against Didius Julianus and marched on Rome in 193 A.D., he secured his political position by coming to an agreement with Clodius Albinus, the governor of Britain. Septimius made Albinus his presumptive successor, gave him the title of Caesar, and struck coins for him in that rank from 193 until the summer of 195.

> The aurei of Clodius Albinus are very rare as a class: only about 20 pieces are known showing him as Caesar.

However, about 18 months after Septimius eliminated his rival, Pescennius Niger, in the East, his agreement with Albinus collapsed. Circa November 195, Albinus proclaimed himself Augustus, crossed from Britain to Gaul, and at Lugdunum proceeded to strike aurei, denarii, and *asses* for himself as emperor. Septimius promptly declared war on Albinus, proclaimed his young son Caracalla as Caesar in Albinus's place, led his army to Gaul, and defeated Albinus in a battle near Lugdunum on February 19, 196.

The exotic reverse type on this aureus of Albinus as Caesar appears to depict Baal Hammon, a Punic god whose worship was brought by the Phoenicians to North Africa, thus supporting the *Historia Augusta*'s statement that Albinus's hometown was Hadrumetum in Punic Africa. Two other depictions of the same god, wearing a cylindrical hat and seated between two sphinxes with his right hand raised, come from Hadrumetum itself. And this type of Albinus belongs to the same early 194 issue as a type of Septimius that shows Hercules and Liber (the patron gods of Septimius's own hometown, Lepcis Magna in Tripolitania), and bears the legend DIS AVSPICIB TR P II COS II P P (Dis Auspicibus Tribunicia Potestas secundum Consul secundum Pater Patriae, meaning "To the Favoring Gods," followed by the titles of the emperor).

The aurei of Clodius Albinus are very rare as a class: only about 20 pieces are known showing him as Caesar, and fewer than five as Augustus. This particular aureus is recorded in four specimens, all from the same die pair. The seated Baal Hammon reverse type is also known on a couple of bronze medallions of Albinus (unfortunately all poorly preserved), and on a unique sestertius of Albinus in Naples.

NOAH'S ARK COIN

ROME · CIRCA 200-250 A.D.

Actual size approx. 35 mm

These coins usually come in worn and corroded condition, but because of their biblical nature they consistently bring between $10,000 and $15,000. The extremely rare specimens in better condition are worth many times those prices.

During the first three centuries A.D., the Roman emperors permitted the cities of the Eastern Roman Empire to produce their own bronze coins. The obverse of these coins commonly portrayed the reigning emperor with his name and titles in Greek circling his head. The reverses bore a great variety of subjects, many of them of local interest. The most exotic and sought after of these coins are the third-century bronze coins of the city of Apameia in Phrygia. These depict the story of Noah's ark from the Hebrew Scriptures.

The city of Apameia was located in western central Anatolia, in present-day Turkey. When it was founded around 270 B.C., Jews were probably among the city's original settlers, and they came to represent a large and prosperous portion of the population. Jews in Greco-Roman Anatolia were usually well integrated into their communities, worked in a wide variety of professions, and even held the highest offices in the local governments. Their religion, and even the stories of the Bible, became familiar to those among whom they lived. Behind Apameia was Mt. Kelainai, where the local Jewish community believed that Noah's ark came to rest. Although the mountain connected with the ark in the modern imagination is Ararat, far to the east of Apameia, the connection is not so obvious in the original Hebrew version of the Bible, where the term *ararat* merely means "mountain." Elsewhere in the ancient world, Jewish communities identified prominent mountains in their own areas as the resting place of the ark. The coin of Apameia was intended to commemorate the local connection to the story of Noah, and it testifies to the large role Jews played in the life of the city.

The Noah's ark coins were struck intermittently from about 200 to about 250 A.D. The obverse always shows the bust and titles of the reigning emperor, Septimius Severus, Macrinus, Gordian III, Philip, or Trebonianus Gallus. On the reverse there is a complex scene. To the right is the ark, which resembles a square box more than a ship. It is labeled "Noah" in Greek, and Noah and his wife look out of the ark while a crow perches on the ark's raised lid. A dove, grasping an olive branch, flies above. To the left, Noah and his wife again appear, arms raised to God in adoration. Encircling the scene of Noah is the name of the local official responsible for the issue, and the name of the city.

The scene requires some explanation. The square, boxy representation of the ark does not agree with the dimensions given in the Bible. Since the Jews and gentiles of Apameia were thoroughly Hellenized, they were familiar with the Hebrew Scriptures through Greek translation. In Greek, the word for "ark" is the same for "chest," and so the ark is shown as a chest. The double representation of Noah and his wife is a convention to express the passage of time. We really have before us two scenes. In the first, Noah and wife peer out of the ark to see the dove return with the olive branch, the first evidence of dry land. In the second, they salute and thank God for their salvation.

Although Noah's ark coins were issued intermittently for half a century, they do not seem to have been struck in large numbers. Only a few, probably less than 20, survive today, and they are eagerly sought by collectors.

SEPTIMIUS SEVERUS AUREUS WITH JULIA AND BOTH SONS

ROME · 202 A.D.

Actual size approx. 20 mm

In 1960, an FDC coin brought SFr 3,100, and in 1972 an Extremely Fine went for SFr 17,000. In 1978 an Extremely Fine brought SFr 45,000. Since then, the prices have stabilized around $20,000 and have not risen because more specimens have entered the market.

In 201 and 202 A.D., Septimius Severus issued his well-known "dynastic" series of aurei and denarii, combining portraits of two or more family members on the same coin.

The simplest reverse types of this series showed the portrait and titles of one family member, and were combined with obverses of another member. Examples of combinations used on these coins include the obverse of Septimius with the reverse of his wife Julia or one of his sons (Caracalla and Geta); the obverse of Julia with the reverse showing Caracalla or Geta; and the obverse of Caracalla with the reverse of Geta or of Plautilla, Caracalla's wife.

Several reverse types included two portraits. Face-to-face portraits of Septimius and Caracalla or of Caracalla and Geta, with the legend AETERNIT IMPERI ("The Eternity of the Empire"), were combined with obverses of all four family members. Jugate portraits of Septimius and Julia with the attributes of the sun and moon, and the legend CONCORDIAE AETERNAE ("To Eternal Harmony"), were combined with obverses of Septimius and Caracalla.

Finally, only aurei showed the whole family on one coin: Septimius on the obverse, and Julia facing between profile busts of Caracalla and Geta on the reverse, with the legend FELICITAS SAECVLI ("The Happiness of the Age"). Our aureus shows this type, on a specimen dated to 202 A.D. by the titles of Septimius on the obverse.

Within the rare class of Severan aurei, the dynastic reverse types of 201 and 202 are comparatively common. Our FELICITAS SAECVLI type, for example, occurs with four different obverse legends of Septimius. A die study of dynastic aurei compiled several decades ago included 46 specimens of this type, from 15 obverse dies and 8 reverse dies.

> To mark his decennalia, Septimius Severus distributed a largesse of 10 aurei per man to the Roman populace.

In 202, to mark his decennalia, Septimius Severus returned to Rome from the East and distributed a largesse of 10 aurei per man to the Roman populace. Perhaps the coins distributed were precisely the dynastic aurei like ours that had been struck in substantial quantity in 201 and 202.

SEPTIMIUS SEVERUS "SHIP IN CIRCUS" AUREUS

ROME · 206 A.D.

Actual size approx. 20 mm

This issue is very popular with collectors. The denarii are only scarce but are so popular they are difficult to find, and there are less than five aurei recorded. In 2002, an aureus brought SFr 80,000 at Numismatica Ars Classica. Today the price would be even higher.

With the legend LAETITIA TEMPORVM ("The Rejoicing of the Times"), this reverse type of Septimius Severus and his sons commemorates the chariot races and animal hunt that took place on the seventh and final day of the Saecular Games of 204 A.D.

According to the surviving inscriptional record of those Saecular Games, the celebration on the seventh day took place in the Circus Maximus and comprised seven chariot races, followed by a hunt of 700 animals (100 each of lions, lionesses, panthers, bears, bison, wild asses, and ostriches). In the coin type, the monuments of the spina, the central barrier around which the chariots raced, prove that the locale is the Circus Maximus: note in particular the obelisk of Augustus in the center, the three cones of the turning post at each end, and pairs of columns supporting seven eggs or seven dolphins that were removed to indicate the laps of a race. The spina has been fitted out to look like a ship, with a sail on the obelisk and added bow, sides, and stern. The chariot races are indicated by the four galloping quadrigas above the spina, and the hunt by the seven animals below it, one each of the seven kinds specified in the inscription: left to right, an ostrich, a lion with a mane, a lioness pursuing a wild ass with long ears, a bison with horns and a hump attacked by a panther, and a bear with a raised head. Although the coin type is dated by a die link and a change in Caracalla's bust type to 206 A.D., there can be no doubt that it commemorates the celebration in the Circus Maximus on the last day of the Saecular Games of 204, two years earlier, as described in the inscription.

This reverse type is extremely rare in gold, being known on just two aurei of Septimius Severus and two of Caracalla.

The historian Dio Cassius describes the hunt of 700 beasts, 100 each of "bears, lionesses, panthers, lions, ostriches, wild asses, bisons," and adds a detail relevant to the coin type: the receptacle in the theater, he says, had been constructed in the shape of a boat, capable of receiving or discharging 400 beasts at once. Due to the carelessness of the Byzantine epitomator whose summary of this section of Dio's work is all that survives, his description of this hunt is tacked onto his description of Severus's decennalian games of 202 A.D. in the available text, but the Saecular Games inscription proves that the hunt in question must actually have taken place two years later, in 204.

This reverse type is extremely rare in gold, being known on just two aurei of Septimius Severus and two of Caracalla. The same type also occurs on rare silver denarii of Septimius Severus, Caracalla, and Geta.

CARACALLA CIRCUS MAXIMUS SESTERTIUS

ROME · 213 A.D.

Actual size approx. 34 mm

In 1932, an Extremely Fine coin brought SFr 200, and in 1987 in a Los Angeles sale the price was $4,250. The price for an Extremely Fine coin is between $15,000 and $20,000 today. The example illustrated here is rarer than the normal in that it is bimetallic, which means it is a two-piece flan, with a brass outer portion into which a copper center piece was inserted before striking. As such, it was a special presentation piece.

Caracalla, along with his brother Geta, became emperor of Rome following the death of their father, Septimius Severus, in 211 A.D. The obverse of this sestertius shows an impressive bust of Caracalla in military dress, surrounded by his name and the titles M AVREL ANTONINVS AVG PIVS BRIT (Marcus Aurelius Antonius Augustus Pius Britannicus).

On the reverse we have more imperial titles and a detailed depiction of the Circus Maximus, as seen from atop the Palatine Hill, showing

- the front wall with its large entrance arch and 11 smaller arches;

- the back wall with spectators, a temple with an altar before it, and the top of an arch surmounted by statues at the right;

- the right-end wall topped by the starter's lodge and statues;

- a triumphal arch surmounted by a statue of Caracalla in a quadriga, at the apex of the rounded left end of the Circus;

- a spina with turning posts at the ends, an obelisk with a statue at its tip in the middle, a statue of Cybele riding a lion, and an apparatus with dolphins for numbering laps;

- four racing chariots, pictured as though just emerging from the starting gates in the arena at the right.

A very similar depiction of the Circus Maximus first appeared on sestertii of Trajan, who probably chose this particular view of the building in order to show off its new western wall, which he had constructed himself, adding 5,000 new seats by building a higher western wall nearer to the base of the Palatine Hill and extending completely over the street that ran there. Caracalla copied the type in 213 A.D., most likely because he himself had also restored the building. One of Caracalla's sestertius reverse dies was later copied on a contorniate die of c. 360, which bore an additional two figures proceeding up the steps of the building carrying sacks that apparently contained a supply of contorniates to be distributed during the games. (Contorniates were coinlike medallions used in late antiquity, possibly as New Year's gifts distributed at games held in December.)

The obverse of this sestertius shows an impressive bust of Caracalla in military dress.

Caracalla's Circus sestertius occurs with two obverse legends, either ending AVG PIVS BRIT as on our coin, or ending PIVS FELIX AVG; there are also several bust-type variants. The type was struck in moderate volume from at least nine different reverse dies. A unique aureus of Caracalla with the Circus type also survives.

650 B.C.   450   250   50   50   250   450   650   850   1050   1250   1450 A.D.

ELAGABALUS AUREUS WITH STONE OF EMESA IN QUADRIGA

ROME · 220 A.D.

Actual size approx. 20 mm

In 1934, a slightly worn example brought SFr 1,250; in 1980, the price was SFr 44,000. In 2004, the price reached SFr 74,750. In more recent sales, that aureus has brought $40,000.

In 217 A.D. the emperor we now call Elagabalus (his official name was Varius Avitus Bassianus Marcus Aurelius Antoninus) was a 13-year-old priest in the Syrian city of Emesa. In that year his grandmother, Julia Maesa, and his mother, Julia Soaemias, both powerful women, successfully conspired with disaffected senators and military officers to overthrow the emperor Macrinus. Once in charge, they spread the word—probably false—that the boy was also the son of the former emperor Caracalla, whom Macrinus had assassinated. Arriving in Rome in 219, Varius brought with him the Stone of Emesa (or had it shipped to Rome before the year ended). This was a black rock, probably a meteorite, that symbolized the Syrian sun god Elagabalus. The young emperor declared Elagabalus the chief deity of the Roman state, built two temples for him in Rome, and himself served as the god's high priest.

Although Elagabalus was emperor for only four years, and only a teenager, he made an indelible impression on Rome—a city that thought it had already seen everything. The stories of his eccentricity and decadence are so numerous that if even only a small percentage of them are true, it would remain unmistakably evident that Elagabalus was totally out of control: he had his chariot pulled by teams of nude women; he dressed as a woman as often as a man; and he was married eight times in four years—three times as a groom and five times as a bride. One of his brides was a Vestal Virgin, a priestess of one of the oldest and most holy temples in Rome, whose votaries were dedicated to perpetual virginity. Elagabalus's conduct outraged the Roman citizens, and on his second attempt to have his cousin Severus

Alexander assassinated, the Praetorian guard assassinated Elagabalus and his mother. His grandmother, Julia Maesa, survived a few years into Severus Alexander's reign and died of old age. After Elagabalus's death, the cult was discontinued and the stone was sent back to Emesa.

Our aureus can be dated to 220 A.D., the year after the emperor and the stone arrived in Rome. It shows the star symbolizing the sun (added to all Roman coins beginning in early 220) in the reverse field, and shares obverse dies with two other reverse types dated to 220 and one type dated to 221. The reverse type calls the sun god CONSERVATOR AVG, "Preserver of the Emperor," and shows the stone being displayed in what appears to be a ceremonial procession. The Greek historian Herodian tells us that in such processions the stone was placed in a chariot drawn by horses, and "no human person sat in the chariot or held the reins, which were fastened to the god as though he were driving himself." The emperor walked backward ahead of the chariot, paying obeisance to the stone and leading the horses.

This aureus is not one of the rarest of the gold coins of Elagabalus. A quick search of museum and auction catalogs turns up 16 specimens, from five obverse dies and four reverse dies. However, the type occurs only on aurei at Rome, not on denarii or bronze coins, so it will be beyond the reach of the average collector. There is also a similar type that occurs on scarce Eastern denarii of Elagabalus. On these the chariot faces right, the sacred stone is shaded by four parasols, and the legend is SANCT DEO SOLI ELAGAB, "To the Holy Sun God Elagabalus."

650 B.C.   450   250   50   50   250   450   650   850   1050   1250   1450 A.D.

PHILIP I MILLENNIAL GAMES COINAGE

ROME · 248 A.D.

Actual size approx. 23 mm

The bronze and silver coins of this celebration are common. The silver cost $100 to $200, and the bronze, depending on type and grade, from $250 to $2,500. The gold is very rare and sells for about $30,000 in Mint State.

Philip I was born Marcus Julius Philippus in the Roman province of Arabia Trachonitis, now part of Syria. Known as Philip the Arab, he was scorned by Roman aristocrats who believed that the outlying provinces produced only ruffians and scoundrels. Nevertheless, Philip managed to maneuver himself to the throne in 244 A.D. by taking advantage of the unstable political climate generated by decades of military and economic instability. Thus it fell to him to plan and orchestrate the festivities marking Rome's millennial year.

Rome's millennial year prompted the reigning emperor, Philip I, to issue commemorative coins.

The Romans calculated their calendar in relation to the year in which they believed their city had been founded, the year known to us as 753 B.C. Thus, the year we call 248 A.D. corresponded to the Roman year 1000 A.U.C. (Ab Urbe Condita, "From the Founding of the City"). Such an anniversary must be celebrated with appropriate grandeur; it prompted the reigning emperor, Philip I, to issue commemorative coins bearing his likeness or that of Empress Otacilia Severa or his son, Philip II.

The obverse of the coin illustrated here depicts the portrait of Philip I surrounded by his name and title, IMP PHILIPPVS AVG, "Emperor Philip Augustus." The reverse shows a cippus, a square column, bearing the inscription COS III, "Consul Three Times," indicating that Philip had held this highest Roman office thrice. Surrounding the cippus is the inscription SAECVLARES AVGG, "Saecular (Centennial) Games of the Emperors." The cippus is a representation of an actual pillar, set up in Rome by Philip I and inscribed with an account of the games.

Philip also issued two other reverse types to commemorate his millennial games. The Temple of Roma type shows the goddess Roma seated in her temple, with the inscription SAECVLVM NOVVM, "The New Age," surrounding. The third issue, produced later in the year, was entirely devoted to the millennial games. It carries the reverse legend SAECVLARES AVGG, but with a number of different animal images, depending on whose portrait graced the obverse. Philip I is paired with a wolf and twins—a reference to the founding of Rome by Romulus and Remus—or with a lion, a stag, or an antelope; Otacilia Severa with a hippopotamus; and Philip II with an elk. Other than the wolf, the animals are thought to represent those killed in the hunt that followed the Games.

650 B.C.   450   250   50   50   250   450   650   850   1050   1250   1450 A.D.

HERENNIA ETRUSCILLA DOUBLE SESTERTIUS

ROME · 250 A.D.

Actual size approx. 40 mm

In 1982 at a Platt sale an Extremely Fine coin brought 92,000 French francs—the same coin that sold in Hess-Leu in 1965 for SFr 3,000. At a Swiss sale in 1981, an Extremely Fine coin brought SFr 31,500. Today the illustrated coin would bring $40,000.

By the middle of the third century A.D., the Roman Empire was in crisis. Emperor after emperor rose and fell in rapid succession—victims of civil wars, assassinations, and the unrestrained greed of the armies. The age of the great Germanic migrations had begun, with tribes pressing eagerly on the northern border, ready to break in at the slightest opportunity. In the east a resurgent Persian empire under the new Sassanid dynasty was equally threatening. Within the empire an unprecedented epidemic swept away many thousands, and uncontrolled inflation devastated the economy. Even during this time of crisis, however, the Roman mint produced striking works of art. One such coin is the double sestertius of Herennia Etruscilla.

This bronze coin was larger than any Rome had issued in 400 years.

Herennia Etruscilla was the wife of Trajan Decius, who had become emperor in 249. Although he ruled only briefly, he is known for his attempts to restore the glory of the empire. Wanting to re-establish traditional Roman values, including the worship of the divine emperors, Trajan launched the first empire-wide persecution of Christians. He also sought to reform the currency, which had declined in both purity and weight. One of these reforms was the introduction of the coin now commonly known as a double sestertius. This bronze coin, larger than any Rome had issued in 400 years, was struck for both Trajan Decius and his wife. Both types are highly sought after by collectors, but that of Herennia is rarer and, many would say, a finer piece of work.

Little is known about Herennia Etruscilla, but her portrait depicts her as a self-possessed, middle-aged woman, a model of Roman virtue and respectability. She wears a diadem in her hair and her bust rests on a crescent moon, indicating her identification with the moon goddess—a common conceit on portraits of imperial ladies in the third century. The legend surrounding her portrait is simple, merely naming her and adding the title Augusta (empress).

The reverse shows the seated figure of Pudicitia, goddess of modesty. The legend reads PVDICITIA AVG (Pudicitia Augusta), clearly referring to the empress. In the exergue are the letters S C, indicating that the coin had been issued with the approval of the Senate, a meaningless tradition by this time.

All of Trajan Decius's grand plans for the reconstruction of the Roman Empire came to nothing. The Goths invaded across the Danube in 251, doing profound damage over a wide area. Initially, Decius's counter-attack went well, but shortly after his elder son Herennius was killed, Decius himself became the first Roman emperor to die in battle. His younger son, Hostilian, was briefly accepted as co-emperor by the succeeding emperor, Trebonianus Gallus, but nothing is known about the fate of his wife, Herennia Etruscilla, whose coins have nevertheless preserved for us fine portraits of a Roman lady living in an age of crisis and anxiety.

650 B.C.   450   250   50   50   250   450   650   850   1050   1250   1450 A.D.

POSTUMUS FACING HEAD AUREUS

ROME · 260–269 A.D.

Actual size approx. 19 mm

The gold aureus may never have come up for sale, but if it did it would probably exceed $250,000. In the 2000 Tkalec sale in Zurich, a copper antoninianus struck from the gold aureus dies sold for SFr 30,000.

The turbulence that held sway in the Roman Empire at the middle of the third century did not end with the deaths of Trajan Decius and Trebonianus Gallus. Convinced that the central government in Rome could not protect them, eastern and northwestern provinces broke away and elevated their own emperors. Postumus, so named because he was born after his father's death, was the western rebel emperor, ruling in Gaul and Britain from 260 until 269.

The quality of Postumus's coinage varies greatly. Many issues are well done, but as his reign progressed and civil war and barbarian incursions took their toll, the style of coins tended to deteriorate and many semi-official and unofficial mints produced strange and sometimes grotesque products. Postumus's gold coinage, however, remained well designed and executed. One issue, known from only two surviving specimens, surpasses all others and is among the finest coins ever struck.

On the obverse of this great coin the emperor Postumus wears the armor and clothing of a Roman general, but he is not depicted in the conventional profile. Instead, he turns to face front, with his shoulders turned slightly toward the right. Postumus's head is turned to the left. His gaze is directed beyond the observer, slightly to the left.

During the mid-third century a new style of portraiture emerged, and the Postumus facing head is a prime example of it. This new portraiture abandoned the earlier norm of showing the subject in calm repose. This was a time that has appropriately been called an "age of anxiety." There was no calm repose. Now the subjects were shown as if glimpsed in a moment of real life, in motion and displaying emotion. Postumus does not smile. He seems strong, even stern, and there is something disquieted and even apprehensive in his face. His hair and beard are treated luxuriously, and his military clothing is shown in fastidious detail. The relief is high, and the proportions and modeling of his face are better than anything that had been done since the height of Greek art in the fifth century B.C., but at the core here is Roman realism, a remarkable study of a man facing crises. The inscription around his head simply proclaims his name and rank, POSTVMVS AVG[ustus].

During the mid-third century a new style of portraiture emerged, and the Postumus facing head is a prime example of it.

On the reverse, Postumus is seated on a curule chair, the chair of judges, high officials, and emperors. Before him kneels a suppliant who raises his hands in appeal to Postumus. The legend, INDVLG PIA POSTVMI AVG, celebrates Postumus's mercy. The scene is well engraved, but cannot compare to the magnificent bust on the obverse.

650 B.C.   450   250   50   50   250   450   650   850   1050   1250   1450 A.D.

GALLIENUS "GALLIENAE AUGUSTAE" AUREUS

ROME · CIRCA 265 A.D.

Actual size approx. 18 mm

This issue is struck on thin flans and often comes damaged. In 1975, a Very Fine example brought SFr 17,000, but more recently these coins have brought $7,500.

Gallienus, who came to the throne in 253 A.D., ruling until 260 with his father Valerian I and then alone until 268, is the only Roman emperor whose name ever appeared on his coins in the feminine form. The obverse legend of our aureus proclaims GALLIENAE AVGVSTAE: "To Galliena Augusta"!

A number of theories have been advanced to explain this anomalous obverse legend. One premise suggests that a usurper struck these coins in mockery of Gallienus's supposed effeminacy. Another proposes that, despite the bearded bust, the coins depict a poorly attested imperial lady Galliena. Yet another posits that the obverse legend is not written in the feminine at all, but simply uses an unusual form of the masculine vocative case, as though addressing Gallienus directly.

One widely accepted possibility is that the coins depict Gallienus as an incarnation of Demeter, the mother-goddess, because he had been initiated into Demeter's Eleusinian Mysteries, the ceremonies for the cult of Demeter and her daughter Persephone, held annually at Eleusis near Athens. If this is so, the name may have been written in the feminine form to honor the goddess. This theory is supported by the fact that the portrait is crowned with a wreath of wheat, the symbol of Demeter, rather than the usual laurel wreath.

It seems likely that Gallienus would have been initiated into the Eleusinian Mysteries. The *Augustan History*, a late Roman collection of biographies, notes that he had served as archon (mayor) of Athens, and had wanted to become an Athenian citizen and participate in all of the local religious ceremonies. The *History* also mentions an inscription preserving an edict of Gallienus relating to the Eleusinian festival. We know, too, that before Gallienus, Hadrian had been initiated into the Eleusinian Mysteries, as attested to by an extraordinary sestertius that depicts his image wreathed with wheat stalks, thus appearing to commemorate the event.

Regardless of the reason behind it, the legend GALLIENAE AVGVSTAE may have been a bit much for the Roman public, for the mint of Rome, while retaining the portrait crowned with the wheat wreath, soon changed the obverse legend to the normal masculine form, GALLIENVS P F AVG. The reverse types remained the same: either the emperor standing left, holding globe and scepter, being crowned by Victory, who stands behind him, with the legend VICTORIA AVG ("the Emperor's Victory"); or Victory riding in a cart drawn right by two horses, with the legend VBIQVE PAX ("Peace Everywhere").

Robert Göbl's comprehensive catalog records 20 Gallienus aurei with the feminine legend and 25 having the same obverse type, but with the masculine legend. The wheat-wreathed portrait was also copied on aurei minted at Siscia, but only with the masculine obverse legend GALLIENVS AVG; of these Göbl knew 18 specimens. One of the Siscian aurei records Gallienus's consular number, VII COS ("Seven Times Consul"), dating the type to 266–268 A.D. and suggesting that Gallienus would have been initiated into the Eleusinian Mysteries in 265 or 266.

CARAUSIUS ET FRATRES SUI ANTONINIANUS

ROME · CIRCA 292–293 A.D.

Actual size approx. 21 mm

In 1969 at the London house Glendining's, a Fine specimen brought £260 (about $620). The same coin at Numismatic Fine Arts later brought $2,000, and the same coin in 1984 at Münzen und Medaillen brought SFr 8,500 (about $20,000). There are many reverse types that combine with this famous obverse, which makes individual varieties elusive, but the issue as a whole is more obtainable than one might think. Today an Extremely Fine coin might bring nearly $10,000.

Carausius was appointed commander of a Roman fleet on the shores of Gaul for the purpose of intercepting seaborne raids of German barbarians. For some reason, he decided to rebel against the central government of Emperor Diocletian and Maximian (Diocletian's lieutenant and emperor of the western two divisions of the empire). Roman sources, reflecting the propaganda of the central government, claim that he had turned pirate, but we need not necessarily believe that. Nevertheless, Carausius sailed to Britain, defeated the government there, and assumed the title of emperor. Diocletian sent Maximian to deal with Carausius, but Carausius repeatedly defeated him and even annexed a considerable portion of Gaul.

This extraordinary and rare coin is like nothing else in all of Roman coinage.

For a brief time, there were peace negotiations between Carausius and Diocletian and Maximian. It was during these negotiations, when it looked as if peace would be achieved, that Carausius issued this extraordinary and rare coin that is like nothing else in all of Roman coinage.

On the obverse we see the three busts of Carausius, Diocletian, and Maximian. The inscription reads CARAVSIVS ET FRATRES SVI ("Carausius and His Brothers"). The reverse repeats the theme, with a depiction of Pax (peace) holding the traditional olive branch, surrounded by the inscription PAX AVGGG, "The Peace of the Three Augusti." The letters that appear in the reverse field are mint control marks.

In the end, the negotiations came to nothing. There is evidence that Diocletian was never serious about making peace with Carausius. While Carausius was occupied with false promises, Diocletian ordered the junior emperor Constantius to build up men and supplies. Constantius then successfully attacked Carausius, taking Boulogne, Carausius's chief strong point in Gaul. Carausius retreated to Britain and prepared to defend the island, but was assassinated by his chief subordinate, Allectus. Allectus failed to mount an effective defense and was quickly swept aside by Constantius, who reunited Britain with the rest of the Roman Empire.

LICINIUS I AND LICINIUS II FACING BUST AUREI

ROME · 321–322 A.D.

Actual size approx. 19 mm

These coins used to bring up to SFr 80,000, but about 12 years ago 30 pieces came onto the market, and sold at that time for $15,000 to $20,000 each. The prices have just begun to rise lately to the point that they are nearer $30,000 for Mint State examples.

Following the retirement of Diocletian, several men vied for control of the Roman world. One of these was Constantine, son of the Constantius whom Diocletian had appointed ruler of Gaul and Britain. Another was Licinius, his brother-in-law. By 313 Constantine was emperor of the west and Licinius was emperor of the east, but civil war erupted between the two. Licinius appointed his four-year-old son, Licinius II, to the throne. In 321 A.D. the two celebrated the boy's quinquennalia, the fifth anniversary of his rule, with elaborate sacrifices to the old Roman gods. These coins were struck in commemoration of that occasion, most likely as gifts for important court officials. In 323 Constantine succeeded in deposing the two after a brief but fierce war. He executed them about a year later.

On the obverse of these aurei we see the facing busts of the two emperors, Licinius I bearded and Licinius II barefaced. Otherwise, they are hardly differentiated. For each, the face is round, the eyes close-set, and the entire face presented not as a model of a living individual but rather as an abstract icon. At first glance, the busts might seem crude, but in fact they are superb examples of the most progressive artistic movement of their day: the shift from realism to abstract idealism. Prior to the beginning of the fourth-century realism, depiction of the world as it actually appears was the standard for Roman art. By the dawn of the fourth century, a new idea had developed: art should not allow itself to be distracted by the "accidents of reality," but should seek to depict its fundamental truths. In the case of an emperor, art should not reflect the ruler's individual appearance, but should show him as an abstract, unblemished being—the gods' chosen ruler on earth. Here the

ruler has become an icon as he faces us, confronting us as we gaze at him. This is an early manifestation of the style that would dominate the Byzantine empire for the next thousand years and would profoundly influence the art of medieval Europe.

The reverse shows Jupiter sitting on an elevated throne holding a long scepter while Victory proffers a laurel wreath. An eagle clasping another wreath stands at the foot of the throne. On the base of the throne is the inscription SIC X/SIC XX, "Thus 10, Thus 20," indicating that the sacrifices just made in thanks for five years of rule would be repeated for 10 and 20 years. The entire depiction is surrounded by the legend IOVI CONS LICINI AVG, "To Jupiter the Protector of Licinius Augustus." There is a variation of this coin that carries the inscription IOVI CONSERVA-TORI CAES, "To Jupiter the Protector of the Caesar," and some specimens, such as the one shown here, show an infant Jupiter on the throne. Mintmarks are in the exergue.

650 B.C.   450   250   50   50   250   450   650   850   1050   1250   1450 A.D.

CONSTANTINOPLE FIVE-SILIQUA COINAGE

ROME · 330 A.D.

Actual size approx. 30 mm

The pair illustrated are the finest known and sold for $125,000 each. Much lesser coins have come up for sale and bring from $10,000 to $20,000.

These five-siliqua silver pieces portray Constantine the Great on the obverse and either Roma (representing the old capital) or Constantinople (representing the new capital) on the reverse. These coins, struck only at the mint of Constantinople, were apparently given out by, or in the presence of, Constantine himself at the dedication ceremony of the city on May 11, 330 A.D. This is the only time that a specific coin can be placed in the presence of a historic individual. The face value of these pieces was very high, and they would have been given only to important persons. Historians surmise that they were distributed in pairs because, while the legend on the Roma reverse begins on the left and continues on the right, on the Constantinople medallion the legend runs from right to left, and also because on later gold issues, Roma and Constantinople are seated together.

The events leading up to the founding of Constantinople and the issuing of these medallions are very interesting. Constantine was born Gaius Flavius Valerius Constantinus in present-day Croatia on February 27, 272 or 273. When his father Constantius died in York, England, in 306, Constantine was proclaimed Augustus by the troops. In the years following the retirement of Diocletian, numerous individuals in addition to Constantine declared themselves emperor and frequently waged war against each other. One such would-be ruler was Maxentius, whom Constantine attacked in the year 312. On the eve of the Battle of the Milvian Bridge on October 28, 312, Constantine had a dream in which Christ told him to make a likeness of the Chi Rho sign that he had seen in the sky two years earlier, and to use it as a defense against attacks by his enemies. Constantine put the sign on his

banners and won the battle. That day marks his unofficial conversion to Christianity, but he was not baptized until shortly before his death (he wanted to go to Heaven without sin). He was buried with 12 empty caskets, signifying that he believed himself to be the 13th apostle.

> This is the only specific coin that can be placed in the presence of a historic individual.

In 324, Constantine was the ruler of the Roman world, but he was displeased by the idea of a pagan senate in Rome. His solution was simple: move the capital of the empire to a new city and create a new Christian senate, leaving the old one to wither in Rome. As the site for the new capital he chose the former Greek city of Byzantium, across the Bosporus from Chrysopolis, where he had defeated Licinius. The rest, of course, is history.

ROMULUS AUGUSTULUS SOLIDUS

ROME · 475-476 A.D.

Actual size approx. 14 mm

In 1925, at a Leo Hamburger sale in Germany, the price was 200 deutsche marks. In 1971 at Münzen und Medaillen, a Very Fine brought SFr 9,300, and at a Sternberg sale in 1973, one made SFr 25,000. The price today is probably $35,000.

By the second half of the fifth century A.D., the eastern half of the Roman Empire was usually ruled by an emperor resident in Constantinople. These eastern emperors either paid little attention to the western half of the empire or treated it with contempt. Much of the western half had been overrun by German tribes. The portion still controlled by the western emperor was mainly restricted to northern Italy, and even that was frequently threatened. After 402 the western emperors usually lived in Ravenna rather than the less defensible Rome.

Romulus was a mere boy, a puppet for his father, and he held virtually no power.

Not all dangers came from the barbarians. The western emperors were totally dependent on their generals to protect them, and the generals exploited their position to become king-makers, murdering and replacing emperors at will. One such general was Orestes, who had been appointed Master of the Soldiers by the emperor Julius Nepos in 475. He promptly revolted and captured Ravenna. Nepos fled for his life, and Orestes installed his son, Romulus, as emperor on October 31, 475.

Romulus was a mere boy, a puppet for his father, and he held virtually no power. Although his official title, like that of every other emperor, was "Augustus," people referred to him as Romulus Augustulus, a pejorative term meaning "the Little Augustus." Julius Nepos, installed on the eastern side of the Adriatic, still claimed he was the legitimate emperor of the West, and neither Zeno nor Basiliscus, two generals fighting to become emperor in the East, would recognize Romulus. The German invaders were an even greater danger. Odoacer, a leader of a mixed troop of German mercenaries, demanded a third of the land in Italy for his men. When Orestes refused, Odoacer captured and executed him and then moved on Ravenna, easily capturing the city. Odoacer took pity on Romulus and merely made him abdicate, giving him an allowance and an estate in southern Italy. He seems to have lived the rest of his life in quiet retirement. So passed from history the last Roman emperor to rule in the West. As T.S. Eliot wrote, "This is the way the world ends: not with a bang, but a whimper."

The surviving coins of Romulus are mainly in gold: a few examples of the standard late-Roman gold coin, the solidus, plus somewhat more gold fractions, or tremisses. On the obverse of the tremissis the emperor faces right, wearing armor and a helmet decorated with a pearl diadem, and carrying a spear and shield. The workmanship is often poor, giving Romulus an unfortunate comic appearance. The somewhat abbreviated Latin legend reads D N ROMVLVS AVGVSTVS P F AVG ("Our Lord Romulus Augustus, Pius, Fortunate, August"). The titles were traditional but sadly inappropriate.

The reverse shows a cross surrounded by a wreath, with the traditional letters CONOB in exergue, indicating that the coin is made of gold as pure as the gold of Constantinople.

JUSTINIAN I FOLLIS

Actual sizes approx. 38 mm (top) and 21 mm

Normally these coins come moderately worn, but Extremely Fine examples sell for $300 to $600, with exceptional coins bringing as much as $1,600.

For many, the coinage reform of the emperor Anastasius (ruled 491–518) marks the beginning of the entity that has been misnamed the Byzantine Empire. While the folles of Anastasius were large, the portraits were in profile and the die work was very crude.

The emperor created a large bronze coin whose obverse was patterned after the gold solidus he was also issuing.

Justinian I, who succeeded his uncle Justin I as emperor, kept to this style for the first 11 years of his reign. In the 12th year, however, something revolutionary happened: the emperor created a large bronze coin whose obverse was patterned after the gold solidus he was also issuing. On this coin, the emperor appears in full armor, facing the viewer, and holding a globus cruciger in his right hand. A legend above gives the emperor's name and titles. The reverse displays a large denominational M with ANNO (year) to the left and XII for the year of his reign to the right. Below the M are the officina letter denoting the workshop group and the mint abbreviation, CON, for Constantinople. These large folles were issued from year 12 of Justinian's reign, which corresponds to 538/539 A.D., until year 15, known to us as

541/542. At that point they began a gradual but noticeable decline in size. The format of these coins remained in use from its inception through the reign of Heraclius, 610 to 641, enjoying a brief resurgence from 668 to 685 during the reign of Heraclius's grandson, Constantine IV.

Justinian folles were struck at every mint in the empire, though only occasionally in some of the more remote corners such as Rome, Ravenna, and Carthage. Relative to the standard of the day, these were medallic, but they were not saved and were circulated as money for hundreds of years, causing them to become quite worn. Thousands of them are still in existence today, but few in perfect condition.

JUSTINIAN II CHRIST SOLIDUS (FIRST REIGN)

BYZANTIUM · 692–695 A.D.

Actual size approx. 21 mm

These coins are only scarce, but again their extreme desirability keeps the prices high. In 1962, an Extremely Fine coin brought SFr 860; by 1976, the price was SFr 4,000, and recently nearly perfect ones have brought $10,000. This issue is often unevenly struck.

Born in 668 or 669 A.D., Justinian II was 16 years of age when he came to the throne upon the death of his father, Constantine IV. He reigned as emperor from July 10, 685, until late in 695, and again from the summer of 705 until November 4, 711. His first reign was marked by cruelty, a penchant for extravagant building projects, and very few worthwhile accomplishments either on the field of battle or in government. In 695, his subjects united behind the general Leontius and Justinian was deposed, mutilated, and exiled to Cherson in the Crimea. Because his nose and tongue were slit by his deposers, Justinian is also known as Justinian Rinotmētos (the Cut-Nosed).

The reason for the mutilation is worthy of note. Byzantine emperors were considered the earthly representatives of both God and Christ, and as such were thought to be impervious to harm. Mutilation, then, was proof of an emperor's desertion by God and Christ, and rendered him unfit to rule. Nevertheless, Justinian was able to build an army while in exile, retake Constantinople, and regain the throne. In his absence, Leontius had himself been deposed by Tiberios III and, upon his return, Justinian lost no time in having both men beheaded. Eventually his tyrannical rule led to another uprising, and this time Justinian, along with his six-year-old son, was murdered.

Be all of that as it may, in the seventh year of his less-than-laudable first reign, Justinian II issued the first coin ever to bear the portrait of Christ. According to the *Catalogue of Byzantine Coins in the Dumbarton Oaks Collection*, by Philip Grierson, the issuance of this coin in 692 may have been in response to publication in that year of Canon 82 of the Quinisext Council in Trullo. This canon decreed that all depictions of either God or Christ be in human form, rather than that of the Paschal Lamb as had previously been required. The theory is supported by the fact that never in the 262 years that Byzantium had been the capital of the Roman Empire had Christ's portrait been depicted on a coin, suggesting that its absence had been caused by a prohibition rather than a lack of desire.

> It was not out of the ordinary for Justinian to have used the statue of Zeus as the model for Christ's face.

The obverse of the solidus shows a majestic portrait of Christ with the bars of a cross emerging from behind his head. Religions commonly influenced one another and often their gods became merged to some degree, so it was not out of the ordinary for Justinian to have used the statue of Zeus by the ancient Greek sculptor Phidias as the model for Christ's face. The emperor himself, wearing imperial robes, laurels, and crown, appears on the reverse. His right hand grasps a cross potent positioned on a three-step base.

JUSTINIAN II CHRIST SOLIDUS (SECOND REIGN)

BYZANTIUM · 705-711 A.D.

Actual size approx. 22 mm

Always scarce, this issue is large and complex, and it is difficult to get a fully struck image. In 1970, they sold for SFr 2,400, which has remained rather constant, meaning that their value has risen along with the Swiss franc. Today these sell for $2,000 to $3,000.

No emperor is ever completely secure on his throne; there are always plots among disgruntled and ambitious subjects. As we have seen, the first reign of Justinian II ended when he was deposed and replaced by his general, Leontius. Subsequently, in 698, Tiberius III deposed Leontius, had his nose slit as Justinian's had been, and sent him to the monastery at Psamathion in Constantinople.

> During his second reign, Justinian produced the second ever portrait of Christ on a coin.

Meanwhile, still in exile, Justinian, having built an army of Bulgars and Slavs, made his way back to Constantinople in 705. When he arrived at the city walls, he was publicly jeered by his former subjects. However, having been raised in the palace, Justinian knew his way around. Under the cover of darkness, he entered the city through its sewer system and appeared on the balcony of the palace the following morning. The amazed inhabitants assumed that if Justinian could magically materialize as he had that morning, he must have been reinstated by God and Christ as their representative on earth. He immediately deposed Tiberius III and had Leontius dragged from his monastery. The two men were taken in chains to the Hippodrome, where Justinian watched chariot races while pressing one foot on the neck of each usurper. After the races, both Leontius and Tiberius were beheaded.

During his second reign, Justinian produced the second ever portrait of Christ on a coin. This bust of Christ was radically different from the first. Though still portrayed with a cross behind his head, this Christ appears as a youthful individual, thought to be Christ the Redeemer, with a closely cut beard, a moustache, and tightly curled hair. He wears a pallium over a colobium. His hand is raised in benediction and he holds a gospel. This obverse is combined with two different reverses, one showing Justinian wearing a loros and a crown, and holding a globus cruciger bearing the word PAX—an ironic inscription given the constant warfare waged during his reign. The second reverse shows a half-length portrait of Justinian wearing a crown and chlamys, accompanied by a half-length figure of his young son Tiberius. Between them they hold a cross potent on a three-step base.

While these gold coins are scarce, they are obtainable. Most are very well preserved, though there are often areas of flat or weak striking.

Justinian's second reign lasted seven years, a period marked by aggression against anyone who had been involved in his overthrow, as well as anyone who could possibly be considered an enemy. It ended with his assassination on November 4, 711.

650 B.C.   450   250   50 50   250   450   650   850   1050   1250   1450 A.D.

JOHN I ZIMISCES ANONYMOUS FOLLIS

BYZANTIUM · 969–1092 A.D.

Actual size approx. 26 mm

There must be close to a million of these coins in existence, but most of them are very worn and worth only about $20. Examples in Extremely Fine are rare and command $500 to $1,000.

In 969 A.D., John I Zimisces became the emperor of the Byzantine Empire. He came from an Armenian family, and the nickname "Zimisces" probably derived from an Armenian word meaning "short." Although of below-average height, John was an active soldier and served as Armenia's governor during the rule of his uncle, Nicephorus II. When Nicephorus eventually deprived him of his command, John retaliated by murdering his uncle and making himself emperor.

During his reign, John I Zimisces made a great innovative change in Byzantine coinage. Before he came to the throne, the follis —the standard copper coin used widely by all levels of society— commonly featured the image and titles of the reigning emperor. John replaced the imperial portrait with a facing bust of Christ. This figure was imposed on a jeweled, nimbate cross, and held a book of the Gospels. The Greek word "Emmanuel" and the Greek abbreviation for "Jesus Christ" appear in the field, to the left and right of the bust, respectively. "Jesus Christ King of Kings" is inscribed in Greek on the reverse. This style of bronze coin would dominate Byzantine bronze coinage from the time of the first issue (in about 970) until 1092. Fourteen major issues, each differing in some degree from the others, were released during this time. Changes involved substitution of a cross for the inscription on the reverse, but an essential similarity existed in that each issue depicted Christ rather than the reigning emperor.

We do not know why John so radically redesigned the bronze coinage, but there are numerous theories. Perhaps the changes reflect the emperor's sense of guilt and repentance about the assassination of his uncle, Nicephorus II. Perhaps they were intended to emphasize the Christian religion of the Byzantines over that of their Muslim enemies. Or perhaps they symbolize the final extinction of what has been called the "iconoclast controversy."

During the eighth and ninth centuries, the iconoclast controversy raged, often violently, throughout the Byzantine Empire. The dispute focused on the theological ideology concerning the display of icons and religious images. Those who supported the use of icons eventually triumphed, and icons were restored in 842, more than a century before John's coinage reform. Despite this, the feud simmered for a long time afterward, and even the emperors were unwilling to reawaken it. By the time John came to the throne, the iconoclast movement was truly dead—perhaps he celebrated this fact by employing Christ's visage on the common coinage of the masses.

John issued millions of the Christ bronze coins, and thousands still exist. Many more were overstruck to produce later varieties, and many of those not overstruck remained in circulation so long that they are very worn. Very few remain in Extremely Fine condition.

In contrast to the copper coinage, the Byzantine gold coinage of this period regularly portrays Christ or Mary on the obverse and the emperor, often with members of his family, on the reverse. Gold coinage did not commonly circulate among the masses, but was largely held by the government and the wealthy. The Byzantine Empire lacked a ready source of silver and issued relatively little silver coinage.

650 B.C. 450 250 50 50 250 450 650 850 1050 1250 1450 A.D.

Actual size approx. 23 mm

Fewer than 15 of these coins are recorded. In 1976, an Extremely Fine coin brought SFr 42,000; in 1985 a Very Fine fetched SFr 25,000. One originally purchased for $15,000 sold in 2005 for $44,850 in the Gemini I sale.

In December of 1041 Michael V Kalapates, the adopted son of the Byzantine empress Zoe, was elevated to the throne by his dying uncle (the second of Zoe's three husbands), Emperor Michael IV. There has been much discussion about whether these coins had, in fact, been issued by the elder Michael, but it now appears virtually certain to have been the younger. It is highly unlikely that after using the same single type for seven years, Michael IV would suddenly decide to change it just before he died.

Michael's reign was short and brutal, lasting only from December 21, 1041, until April 13, 1042, but he left behind a magnificent and unique coin type.

Michael V began his reign under the regency of the old empress Zoe, but he quickly put an end to that arrangement and took the government into his own hands. It seems that the ungrateful Michael was so resentful of Zoe that he issued this coin—an entirely new type without any family reference at all—to assert his independence. He then exiled both Zoe and his uncle

John, a eunuch who had been the administrator of his father's court. This last action so inflamed the people of Constantinople that they fought back with an insurrection that left 3,000 dead and deposed Michael V after a reign of only about four months. Zoe returned and ruled jointly with her sister Theodora for less than two months, from April 21 to June 12, 1042, when she found a new husband, Constantine IX, who ruled for the next 13 years in their stead.

Michael's reign was short and brutal, lasting only from December 21, 1041, until April 13, 1042, but he left behind a magnificent and unique coin type. The obverse depicts Christ sitting on a backless throne, his right hand raised in benediction and his left hand holding a book of the Gospels on his lap. On the left side of the distinctive reverse, the archangel Michael stands facing, wearing a chlamys. Michael V, wearing a crown with pendilia and a loros, stands right. They hold a labarum between them. To Michael's right the hand of God comes forth to crown him. There are fewer than 15 of these wonderful coins recorded.

CONSTANTINE XI STAVRATON

BYZANTIUM · 1453 A.D.

Actual size approx. 23 mm

In the late 1980s, about 90 coins of Constantine XI came to market. Three major museums in this field of study purchased specimens, and three more were put up for auction. The lowest price for a stavraton was $6,000 and the highest $15,000. Some of these coins have come to auction again as their purchasers have died or retired. In the Gemini II sale in 2006, one of the coins brought $20,700.

The history of the last years of the Byzantine Empire, as the Eastern Roman Empire is sometimes incorrectly called, is a series of remarkable and seemingly contradictory events. When the emperor John VIII died, his brothers Constantine and Demetrius both claimed the throne. The family went to Murad II, sultan of the Ottomans, to decide who would become the new Byzantine emperor. Murad chose Constantine, who was crowned in January 1449 as Constantine XI.

On arriving in Constantinople (all that remained of the empire), Constantine XI found the city in terrible financial shape. To raise money, he asked the Ottomans for a large increase in payments to maintain in exile in Constantinople the Ottoman Orchan Effendi, a potentially dangerous rival to Sultan Muhammad II, who had succeeded Sultan Murad. Upon hearing the request, Ottoman grand vizier Chalil Pasha, a Christian, flew into a rage and persuaded Muhammad II to take the city. Interestingly, Muhammad was raised by his father's last wife, a Christian, Maria Brankovich of Serbia. After Murad II's death, Constantine XI proposed marriage to her, but his offer was declined. Another odd fact is that during the siege, while 7,000 Christians were defending the city, 30,000 Christians were fighting with the Muslims of the Ottoman Empire. This remarkable set of circumstances shows the world is not black and white but shades of gray.

Until 1974, no coins of Constantine XI had ever been identified. In that year, the great Byzantine scholar Simon Bendall discovered the first one, and found that one other had been misidentified a year earlier as a coin of John VIII. Not long after, 90 more coins of Constantine XI became known. While some of these were struck for Constantine's coronation, most were issued during the siege of Constantinople by the Ottoman king Muhammad II. This siege would lead to the fall of Constantinople and the end of the final remnant of the Roman Empire.

We know that most of the coins of Constantine XI were siege coins because the portrait of the emperor is of extraordinary crude workmanship, while the bust of Christ on the obverse is, by contrast, quite good. The Byzantines considered themselves to be ruled by an emperor who was God's and Christ's representative on earth. One always knew that Christ would be a constant on the obverse of the coin but did not know who the emperor might be in the future. The dies for Christ's portraits were prepared before the siege. During the siege, many paid employees of the empire, now a mere city, deserted because of the dire financial straits in Constantinople. The situation was so bad that the obverse dies that bore the portrait of the emperor were cut by unqualified die cutters.

Among those who left the city was its cannon maker, who went to the side of the Ottomans and made a cannon that battered the city walls every day. Every night the workmen would repair the city walls—but not until they were paid. The only way to pay them was to melt the silver vessels in Hagia Sophia and the city's other churches to create these crude but very important and now historic coins. The cannon ultimately did not end the siege, however. Perhaps by accident, perhaps through bribery, someone neglected to lock a sally port (a small, easily secured door in a fortified wall), and the Ottoman forces entered the city. Constantine XI was killed in the fighting, but pious legend claims that the wall of the great church, Hagia Sophia, opened behind the altar and he entered the opening, which closed behind him. According to the legend, it will remain closed until the day Constantine emerges to reestablish the empire.

650 B.C.   450   250   50   50   250   450   650   850   1050   1250   1450 A.D.

APPENDIX AND
COLLECTOR RESOURCES

This gallery illustrates each of the coin types ranked in *100 Greatest Ancient Coins*.
The coins are all shown here at actual size, to give the reader a sense of their scale relative to each other.

**Ionia Electrum
Stater
(page 9)**

**Ephesus Phanes Electrum
Stater
(page 10)**

**Ephesus Phanes Electrum
Stater
(page 10)**

**Poseidonia
Stater
(page 11)**

THE COINAGE OF CROESUS

**Prototype Heavy Gold
Stater
(page 12; 10.73g)**

**Heavy Gold
Stater
(page 13; 10.76g)**

**Light Gold
Stater
(page 13; 8.07g)**

**Light Persian Gold
Stater
(page 13; 8.06g)**

**Heavy 1/3 Gold
Stater
(page 13; 3.55g)**

**Light 1/3 Gold
Stater
(page 13; 2.67g)**

**Heavy 1/6 Gold
Stater
(page 13; 1.77g)**

**Light 1/6 Gold
Stater
(page 13; 1.36g)**

**Heavy 1/12 Gold
Stater
(page 13; 0.89g)**

**Light 1/12 Gold
Stater
(page 13; 0.68g)**

**Light 1/12 Gold
Stater
(page 13; 0.68g)**

**Light 1/12 Gold
Stater
(page 13; 0.67g)**

**Light 1/12 Gold
Stater
(page 13; 0.66g)**

**Heavy 1/24 Gold
Stater
(page 13; 0.42g)**

**Light 1/24 Gold
Stater
(page 13; 0.33g)**

**First Prototype
Silver Stater
(page 13; 10.41g)**

Second Prototype Silver
Stater
(page 13; 10.67g)

Second Prototype Silver
Stater
(page 13; 10.64g)

Silver Stater
First Regular Issue
(page 13; 10.68g)

Silver Stater
Second Regular Issue
(page 13; 10.74g)

Second Prototype
Silver Siglos
(page 13; 5.23g)

Silver Siglos
First Regular Issue
(page 13; 5.33g)

Silver Siglos
Second Regular Issue
(page 13; 5.35g)

Silver 1/3
Stater
(page 13; 3.55g)

Silver 1/6
Stater
(page 13; 1.75g)

Silver 1/12
Stater
(page 13; 0.88g)

Silver 1/12
Stater
(page 13; 0.87g)

Silver 1/16
Stater
(page 13; 0.64g)

Silver 1/24
Stater
(page 13; 0.44g)

Silver 1/24
Stater
(page 13; 0.43g)

Silver 1/24
Stater
(page 13; 0.40g)

Cyzicus Electrum
Stater
(page 14)

Cyzicus Electrum
Stater
(page 14)

Alexander I of Macedonia
Octodrachm
(page 15)

Syracuse Alpheios Facing
Head Tetradrachm
(page 16)

Delphic
Tridrachm
(page 17)

Aetna
Tetradrachm
(page 18)

Cos Discus Thrower
Stater
(page 19)

Syracuse Demareteion
Decadrachm
(page 20)

Athens
Decadrachm
(page 22)

Naxos
Tetradrachm
(page 24)

Aegina Sea Turtle
Stater
(page 26)

Aegina Sea Turtle
Stater
(page 26)

Cnossus Minotaur
Stater
(page 27)

Athens
Tetradrachm
(page 28)

Thebes
Stater
(page 30)

Thebes
Stater
(page 30)

Melos
Stater
(page 31)

Acragas Skylla
Tetradrachm
(page 32)

Zeus Olympic
Stater
(page 33)

Kimon
Decadrachm
(page 34)

Kimon
Decadrachm
(page 34)

Kimon
Decadrachm
(page 35)

Euainetos
Decadrachm
(page 36)

Arethusa Facing Head
Tetradrachm by Kimon
(page 38)

Camarina
Didrachm
(page 40)

Gela
Tetradrachm
(page 41)

Acragas
Decadrachm
(page 42)

Larissa
Drachm
(page 44)

Syracuse Arethusa
100-Litra Coin
(page 45)

Carthaginian Dido
Tetradrachm
(page 46)

Clazomenae
Tetradrachm
(page 47)

Rhodes
Tetradrachm
(page 48)

Rhodes
Tetradrachm
(page 48)

Amphipolis
Tetradrachm
(page 49)

Philip II
Tetradrachm
(page 50)

Metapontum
Stater
(page 51)

Panticapaeum Gold
Stater
(page 52)

Tarentum Horseman
Stater
(page 53)

Tarentum Gold
Stater
(page 54)

Alexander the Great
Tetradrachm
(page 55)

Corinth
Stater
(page 56)

Alexander the Great
Porus Decadrachm
(page 57)

Lysimachus
Tetradrachm
(page 58)

Demetrius Poliorcetes
Tetradrachm With
Nike on Prow
(page 59)

Aes Grave
As
(page 60)

Pergamon Gold
Stater
(page 61)

Arsinoë II Gold
Octodrachm
(page 62)

Ptolemy III Dynastic
Octodrachm
(page 63)

Berenike II
Dodecadrachm or
Pentadecadrachm
(page 64)

Hannibal
Coin
(page 65)

Oath-Taking
Stater
(page 66)

40-*As*
Gold Coin
(page 67)

Flamininus Gold
Stater
(page 68)

Pharnaces I of Pontus
Tetradrachm
(page 69)

Perseus "Zoilos" Silver
Tetradrachm
(page 70)

Eucratides I
Heroic Bust
Coin
(page 71)

Orophernes Silver
Tetradrachm
(page 72)

Sulla
Aureus
(page 73)

Cleopatra VII Ascalon
Mint Tetradrachm
(page 74)

Caesar Portrait
Denarius
(page 75)

Sulla's Dream
Denarius
(page 76)

Octavian and Julius
Caesar Aureus
(page 77)

Brutus "Eid Mar"
Denarius
(page 78)

Quintus Labienus
Aureus
(page 80)

Sextus Pompey
Aureus
(page 81)

Cleopatra and Mark
Antony Portrait Denarius
(page 82)

Augustus Cistophorus
With Sphinx Reverse
(page 83)

Augustus Facing Portrait
Denarius
(page 84)

Tiberius Denarius
(Biblical Tribute Penny)
(page 85)

Jerusalem Tyrian-Type
Shekel
(page 86)

Caligula Three Sisters
Sestertius
(page 87)

Britannicus
Sestertius
(page 88)

Nero Port of Ostia
Sestertius
(page 89)

Clodius Macer Portrait
Denarius
(page 90)

First Revolt Year 5
Shekel
(page 91)

Vespasian "Judea Capta"
Sestertius
(page 92)

Titus Colosseum
Sestertius
(page 93)

Trajan Danube Bridge
Sestertius
(page 94)

Hadrian Year 874 of
Rome Aureus
(page 95)

Bar Kochba Year 1
Tetradrachm
(page 96)

Antoninus Pius
Labors of Hercules
Drachm
(page 97)

Antoninus Pius
Labors of Hercules
Drachm
(page 97)

Commodus Portrait
Sestertius With Lion Skin
of Hercules
(page 98)

Clodius Albinus
Aureus
(page 99)

Noah's Ark
Coin
(page 100)

Septimius Severus
Aureus With Julia and
Both Sons
(page 101)

Septimius Severus
"Ship in Circus"
Aureus
(page 102)

Caracalla Circus
Maximus Sestertius
(page 103)

Elagabalus Aureus With
Stone of Emesa in Quadriga
(page 104)

Philip I
Millennial Games
(page 105)

Herennia Etruscilla
Double Sestertius
(page 106)

Postumus Facing Head
Aureus
(page 107)

Gallienus "Gallienae
Augustae" Aureus
(page 108)

Carausius et Fratres
Sui Antoninianus
(page 109)

Licinius I Facing Bust
Aureus
(page 110)

Licinius II Facing Bust
Aureus
(page 110)

Constantinople
Five-Siliqua
(page 111)

Romulus Augustulus
Solidus
(page 112)

Justinian I
Follis
(page 113)

Justinian I
Follis
(page 113)

Justinian II Christ
Solidus (First Reign)
(page 114)

Justinian II Christ
Solidus (Second Reign)
(page 115)

John I Zimisces
Anonymous Follis
(page 116)

Michael V
Coin
(page 117)

Constantine XI
Stavraton
(page 118)

aes grave *as*—large bronze coin of the Roman Republic weighing about 270 grams.

amphora—vase, usually of unglazed terra-cotta, with handles on either side and a long neck narrower than the body; generally used for storage.

ampyx—headband (often of metal) used for binding the front hair.

anepigraphic—without inscription.

antoninianus—coin used during the Roman Empire valued at two denarii.

archon—Greek word meaning "ruler," frequently employed as the title of some specific public office.

Arethusa—in Greek mythology, a nymph and an attendant to Artemis; depicted on decadrachms of Syracuse.

as (*pl.* **asses**)—bronze coin of the Roman Republic and copper coin of the Roman Empire.

Asclepius—Greek god of healing and medicine.

Athena—Greek goddess of wisdom and war; analogous to the Roman goddess Minerva.

Attic weight—coin weight value system of ancient Greece, in which the tetradrachm weighed approximately 17.2 grams.

augur—priest and official of ancient Rome who interpreted the will of the gods by studying the flight of birds.

aureus (*pl.* **aurei**)—standard gold coin of the Roman Empire and Republic.

Battle of Marathon—battle instigated by King Darius I of Persia against the Greeks in 490 B.C. to secure the western part of Greece.

Boeotian shield—type of shield with side openings; often accompanies mythic Greek heroes in art.

censor—Roman magistrate responsible for maintaining the census, public morality, and various financial duties.

chlamys—short military cloak of ancient Greece, Rome, and Byzantium.

cippus—squared stone pillar, usually bearing a commemorative inscription and set up as a monument or boundary marker.

Circus Maximus—ancient arena and mass entertainment venue in Rome.

cistophorus (*pl.* **cistophori**)—silver coin of Asia Minor, so called because it commonly bore the design of a cista mystica (a sacred chest); also a Roman silver coin equivalent to three denarii.

college of augurs—one of the four great religious corporations of Roman priests.

colobium—blouse or sleeveless coat.

consul—highest elected office in the Roman Republic and an appointed office in the Roman Empire.

contorniate—bronze medallion with a deep furrow on the contour edge, struck from about 360 to 425 A.D.

cornucopia—horn of plenty; a symbol of prosperity dating to the fifth century B.C.

corpus—complete body of knowledge on a single subject.

cross potent—cross with a crossbar on each arm.

cuirass—leather or metal piece of armor covering the body from neck to waist.

curule—chair occupied by a high official of ancient Rome.

daric—gold coin used in the Persian empire.

decadrachm—ancient Greek silver coin worth 10 drachms.

decennalia—celebration marking a ruler's 10th year on the throne.

Delian League—association of Greek city-states led by Athens during the fifth century B.C.

denarius (*pl.* **denarii**)—basic silver coin of the Roman Empire.

diadem—headband, wreath, or crown symbolizing royalty; also, an ornamental headpiece or tiara.

didrachm—ancient Greek coin worth two drachms.

Dioscuri—usually referred to as Castor and Pollux; in Greek mythology, twin sons of Zeus and Leda.

dodecadrachm—large ancient Greek coin worth 12 drachms.

drachm—ancient Greek coin and basic monetary unit; originally the amount of bronze rods that could be grasped in the hand.

dupondius (*pl.* **dupondii**)—Roman coin, usually of brass, worth two *asses*.

Edoni—race of people who lived in southern Thrace.

electrum—natural alloy of gold and silver, used to mint early coins in ancient times.

exergue—line on the reverse of a coin below the central part of the design, under which the mint name was frequently located.

flan—planchet, or blank piece of metal, from which a coin is struck.

follis (*pl.* **folles**)—bronze coin put into circulation during the coinage reform of the emperor Diocletian. It remained in circulation until the 12th century.

fourrée—base-metal coin with a plating of precious metal, usually of silver over a copper core; some were created as counterfeits, while others were issued by the official mint.

globus cruciger—orb topped with a crucifix; a Christian symbol of authority.

gorgon—in Greek mythology, a female monster with hair of living snakes, the sight of which would turn the viewer to stone; Medusa is the most famous.

greaves—armor pieces that cover the shins.

Helots—serfs of Sparta who were tied to the land and could be freed only by the state.

Hera—in Greek mythology, a goddess married to Zeus; queen of the Greek deities; analogous to the Roman goddess Juno.

Heracles—in Greek mythology, a divine hero, son of Zeus; known for his 12 labors, he was the mythological archetype for human fortitude and bravery. Also known by his Roman name, Hercules.

Hipparis—one of two rivers at Camarina, an ancient city on the south coast of Sicily. Oanus is the second river.

incuse—coin design that has been impressed below the coin's surface, that appears on the reverse of Archaic and early classical Greek coins.

janiform—having two faces looking in opposite directions, like the god Janus.

Janus—Roman god of gates and doorways; depicted with two faces looking in opposite directions.

jugate—paired or connected; in coins, a design in which two portraits are overlapped with both faces clearly visible.

Juno—in Roman mythology, queen of the gods, wife of Jupiter, and mother of Mars; analogous to the Greek goddess Hera.

Jupiter—supreme deity in the Roman pantheon of gods; equivalent to the Greek god Zeus.

labarum—military standard, first used by the Roman emperor Constantine I, that displayed the first two Greek letters of the word "Christ" (chi and rho).

laureate—crowned with a laurel wreath.

litra—Greek unit of mass (about .72 pounds).

lituus—instrument used by Roman augurs in their rituals; also used to symbolize the office of augur.

loros—long scarf, especially the jeweled one worn on festive occasions by emperors.

Mars—Roman god of war; analogous to the Greek god Ares.

mill-sail pattern—design used as an incuse on Archaic Greek coins in Aegina.

mole—massive work formed of masonry or large stones in the sea as a pier or breakwater.

moneyer—authorized minter of coins.

Nike—Greek goddess of victory; analogous to the Roman goddess Victory.

nimbate—having a nimbus or halo, a luminous vapor appearing around a god or goddess when on earth.

nomos (*pl.* **nomoi**)—ancient Greek silver stater.

obverse—front of a coin.

octodrachm—ancient coin worth eight drachms; usually a gold coin issued in Egypt by the Ptolemaic Greek rulers.

officina—workshop within a mint.

pallium—ecclesiastical vestment consisting of a cloth band or scarf worn around the neck and shoulders and ornamented with crosses.

parazonium—dagger or short sword, used as a last line of defense by Greek warriors.

Peloponnesian War—war fought between Athens and Sparta from 431 to 404 B.C.

pendilia—pendants hanging from either side of a crown.

pentadecadrachm—ancient Greek coin worth 15 drachms.

Persian Wars—series of conflicts (499–478 B.C.) between the Persian Empire and several Greek city-states; in particular, the two Persian invasions of Greece in 490 B.C. and 480–479 B.C., both of which were repelled.

Phrygian cap—soft conical hat given to freed slaves during the Roman Empire; thus, a symbol of freedom.

planchet—blank piece of metal that becomes a coin when struck with a die.

pontifex—member of the highest council of priests in ancient Rome.

Ptolemaic weight—coin weight value system of ancient Egypt, in which the tetradrachm weighed approximately 14.2 grams.

Punic Wars—series of three wars fought between Rome and Carthage between 264 B.C. and 146 B.C.

quadriga—chariot drawn by four horses; frequently found as a design on tetradrachms.

quaestor—in ancient Rome, an important public official, who might be responsible for prosecuting criminals, administering the treasury, or serving as paymaster for the military.

quinquennalia—celebration marking a ruler's fifth year on the throne.

reverse—back of a coin.

Rhodian weight—coin weight value system of ancient Rhodes, in which the tetradrachm weighed approximately 15.2 grams.

rhyton—ancient ceremonial drinking vessel, sometimes in the form of the head of an animal, a person, or a mythological being; usually made of glazed terra-cotta, but sometimes of gold or, less frequently, silver.

sally port—small, easily secured door in a fortified wall.

sestertius (*pl.* **sestertii**)—small silver coin of the Roman Republic; later, a large coin of bronze, brass, or the alloy orichalcum, and a basic denomination of imperial Rome.

shekel—ancient unit of weight and currency. In coin form, a silver shekel weighed approximately 14.2 grams.

siglos—standard ancient Persian silver coin.

Silenus—in Greek mythology, the tutor and advisor of Dionysus; more generally, any of a number of drunken followers of Dionysus.

siliqua—late Roman silver coin.

Skylla—destructive female sea monster in Greek mythology.

solidus—ancient Roman gold coin introduced by Constantine and weighing 4.45 grams; generally considered a Byzantine denomination.

Sparta—militaristic city-state of ancient Greece.

sphinx—mythological creature depicted on ancient Greek and Roman coins as having the body of a lion and the breast and head of a woman.

spina—low wall in the center of a Circus, around which chariots raced.

splendone—headdress, similar to a diadem, worn by Greek women.

stater—ancient Greek coin of silver or gold. The silver and gold coins are not related to each other.

stavraton (*pl.* **stavrata**)—Byzantine silver coin.

stoa—ancient Greek portico.

taenia—headband of the classical period.

Tanit—patron goddess of Carthage, identified with the moon, fertility, and motherhood.

tetradrachm—as a Greek coin, a silver coin worth four drachms; as a Roman coin, debased with those of Roman Egypt under Diocletian, a small, thick bronze coin.

Thebes—powerful ancient Greek city-state located in Boeotia.

togate—wearing a toga.

totem bird—in Greek mythology, a supernatural bird (such as the one owned by the goddess Athena) that aids or advises.

travertine—sedimentary rock used in construction.

tribunician—pertaining to tribunes.

tribute penny—biblical phrase referring to the Tiberius denarius; the term came into use with the King James translation of the Bible, because in James I's England a penny was a silver coin.

trident—three-pronged staff or spear, as carried by the sea god Poseidon (Roman analogue: Neptune) or used in ancient Roman gladiatorial combats.

triskele—figure with three curved forms (such as bent human legs) radiating from a center.

trite—ancient Greek denomination, one-third of an electrum stater.

triumvir—one member of a ruling body of three, such as the First Triumvirate.

Victory—Roman goddess of victory; analogous to the Greek goddess Nike.

Wappenmünzen—German term (literally, "coat-of-arms coins") for the earliest coinage of Athens (c. sixth century), which features designs once thought to be coats of arms.

Zeus—Greek king of the gods; analogous to the Roman god Jupiter or Jove.

Alföldi, A. *The Portrait of Caesar on the Denarii of 44 B.C. and the Sequence of the Issues.* Centennial publication of the American Numismatic Society. New York, 1958.

Arnold-Biucchi, Carmen, and Arnold-Peter C. Weiss. "The River God Alpheios on the First Tetradrachm Issue of Gelon at Syracuse." *Quaderni Ticinesi: Numismatica e Antichita' Classiche,* 36 (2007).

Bellinger, Alfred R., and Philip Grierson, eds. *Catalogue of the Byzantine Coins in the Dumbarton Oaks Collection and in the Whittemore Collection.* 5 vols. Washington, DC: Dumbarton Oaks, 1968–1999.

Berk, Harlan J. "The Coinage of Croesus: Another Look." *Journal of the Society for Ancient Numismatics* 20, no. 1 (1997): 14–15.

———. "The Coinage of Croesus: New Type Supports Traditional Theories." *The Celator* 4, no. 10 (October 1990): 6.

———. *Eastern Roman Successors of the Sestertius.* Joliet, IL: 1988.

———. "Die Münzprägung des Kroisos." *Münzen Revue* (September 1997): 30–32.

———. *Roman Gold Coins of the Medieval World, 383–1453 A.D.* Joliet, IL: 1986.

Boehringer, Erich. *Die Münzen von Syrakus.* Berlin: Walter de Gruyter, 1929.

Bopearachchi, Osmund. *Monnaies greco-bactriennes et indo-grecques.* Paris: Bibliothèque Nationale, 1991.

Brett, Agnes Baldwin. *Catalogue of Greek Coins.* Boston: Museum of Fine Arts, 1955.

Burnett, Andrew. *Coinage in the Roman World.* London: Seaby, 1987.

Cahn, Herbert A. *Die Münzen der Sizilischen Stant Naxos.* Basel: Borkhauser, 1944.

Calico, Xavier E. *The Roman Aurei.* Vols. 1 and 2. Barcelona: X. and F. Calico, 2003.

Carradice, Ian, and Martin Price. *Coinage in the Greek World.* London: Seaby, 1988.

Catalogue of Greek Coins in the British Museum. 29 vols. London: British Museum, 1873–1927.

Cohen, Henry. *Description historique des monnaies frappées sous l'Empire romain.* 8 vols. Paris, 1880–1892.

Coins of the Roman Empire in the British Museum. 6 vols. London: British Museum, 1923–1962.

Crawford, Michael. *Roman Republican Coinage.* 2 vols. Cambridge University Press, 1974.

Fischer-Bossert, Wolfgang. *Chronologie der Didrachmenprägung von Tarent.* Berlin: Walter de Gruyter, 1999.

Foss, Clive. *Roman Historical Coins.* London: Seaby, 1990.

Gallatin, Albert. *Syracusan Decadrachms of the Euainetos Type.* Cambridge, MA: Harvard University Press, 1930.

Göbl, Robert. *Dokumente zur Geschichte der iranischen Hunnen in Baktrien und Indien.* 4 vols. Wiesbaden: Otto Harrassowitz, 1967.

Grierson, Philip, and Melinda Mays. *Catalogue of Late Roman Coins in the Dumbarton Oaks Collection.* Washington, DC: Dumbarton Oaks, 1992.

Grosse, S.W. *Catalogue of the McClean Collection of Greek Coins.* Cambridge University Press, 1923.

Grueber, H.A. *Coins of the Roman Republic in the British Museum.* 3 vols. London, 1910.

Hahn, Wolfgang. *Moneta Imperii Byzantini.* 3 vols. Vienna: Verlag der Österreichischen Akademie der Wissenschaften, 1973–1981.

Head, Barclay V. *Historia Numorum: A Manual of Greek Numismatics.* Oxford University Press, 1911.

Hendin, David. *Guide to Biblical Coins.* 4th ed. New York: Amphora Books, 2001.

Jameson, R. *Monnaies grecques antiques.* Paris: Feuardent Freres, 1913.

Jenkins, G. Kenneth. *Ancient Greek Coins.* 2nd ed. London: Spink and Son, 1990.

———. *The Coinage of Gela.* Berlin: Walter de Gruyter, 1970.

———. "Coins of Punic Sicily: Carthage Series." *Schweizrische Numismatische Rundschau* 57 (1978): 5–68.

Jongkees, J.H. *The Kimonian Dekadrachms.* Utrecht: Kemink on Zoon, 1941.

King, C.E., and David J. Sear. *Roman Silver Coinage.* Volume 5, *Carausius to Romulus Augustus.* London: Seaby, 1987.

Kraay, Colin. *Archaic and Classical Greek Coins.* London: Methuen, 1976.

Kraay, Colin, and Max Hirmer. *Greek Coins.* London: Thames and Hudson, 1966.

Lorber, Catherine C. "The Early Facing Head Drachms of Thessalian Larissa." In *Florilegium Numismaticum Studia in Honorem U. Westermark,* edited by H. Nilsson, 259–282. Stockholm: Svenska Numismatika Foreningen, 1992.

Mattingley, Harold. *Roman Coins: From the Earliest Times to the Fall of the Western Empire.* 1928. Reprint, New York: Sanford J. Durst, 1986.

Mattingley, Harold, Edward A. Sydenham, et al. *Roman Imperial Coinage.* 10 vols. London: 1923–1994.

Melville-Jones, John. *A Dictionary of Ancient Greek Coins.* London: Seaby, 1986.

———. *A Dictionary of Ancient Roman Coins.* London: Seaby, 1990.

Meshorer, Ya'akov. *A Treasury of Jewish Coins.* New York: Amphora Books, 2001.

Mijatovich, Chedomil. *Constantine Palaeologus: The Last Emperor of the Greeks, 1448–1453.* Chicago: Argonaut, 1892.

Milbank, Samuel R. *The Coinage of Aegina.* Numismatic Notes and Monographs, no. 24. New York: American Numismatic Society, 1925.

Morkholm, Otto. *Early Hellenistic Coinage: From the Accession of Alexander to the Peace of Apamea (336–188 B.C.).* London: Spink and Son, 1991.

Plant, Richard J. *Greek Coin Types and Their Identification.* London: Seaby, 1979.

Price, Martin. *The Coinage in the Name of Alexander the Great and Philip Arrhidaeus: A British Museum Catalogue.* London: British Museum, 1991.

Price, Martin, and Nancy Waggoner. *Archaic Greek Silver Coinage: The "Asyut" Hoard.* London: V.C. Vecchi and Sons, 1975.

Ravel, Oscar E. *Catalogue of Tarentine Coins Formed by M.P. Vlasto.* London: Spink and Son, 1947.

Seaby, H.A. *Roman Silver Coins.* 4 vols. Revised by David R. Sear and Robert Loosley. London: Seaby, 1978–1982. Originally published 1952–1971.

Sear, David R. *Greek Coins and Their Values.* 2 vols. London: Spink and Son, 1997 and 1998.

———. *The History and Coinage of the Roman Imperators, 49–27 B.C.* London: Spink and Son, 1988.

Seltman, Charles. *Greek Coins: A History of Metallic Currency and Coinage Down to the Fall of the Hellenistic Kingdoms.* London: Methuen, 1933.

———. *Masterpieces of Greek Coinage.* Oxford: Bruno Cassirer, 1949.

———. *Temple Coins of Olympia.* Cambridge: Bowes and Bowes, 1921.

Starr, Chester G. *Athenian Coinage 480–449 B.C.* Oxford University Press, 1970.

Sutherland, C.H.V. *Roman Coins.* New York: Putnam, 1974.

Svoronos, J.N. *Münzen der Ptolemäer.* Athens, 1904.

Sydenham, Edward A. *The Coinage of the Roman Republic.* London: Spink and Son, 1952.

Sylloge Nummorum Graecorum: The Royal Collection of Coins and Medals, Danish National Museum. 43 vols. 1942–1977.

Tudeer, Laurel O. *Tetradrachmenprägung von Syrakus.* Berlin, 1913.

Weidauer, Liselotte. *Probleme der frühen Elektronprägung.* Fribourg, Switzerland: Office du Livre, 1945.

Westermark, Ulla, and Kenneth Jenkins. *The Coinage of Kamarina.* London: Royal Numismatic Society Special Publication number 9, 1980.

ABOUT THE AUTHOR

Harlan J. Berk started his career as did many numismatists of his time: through a boyhood interest in coins. In 1949 his grandmother gave him a handful of Indian Head cents and a Swedish medal dated 1818. A few years later he discovered a 1916-D dime in his weekly allowance, and found when he consulted a 1954 Whitman Blue Book that it was worth $12.50. Coin collecting became numismatics, and it just got more interesting from there.

At age 22, he was hired just out of college as the coin expert in a leased department (owned by a boyhood friend of Norman Stack's) in the Carson Pirie Scott department store in Chicago. Harlan founded his own company, Harlan J. Berk Ltd., in late 1964; he now runs it with two of his children, Aaron and Shanna. He is also president and part owner of Gemini LLC, a numismatic auction firm.

Harlan has been a member of the Professional Numismatists Guild (PNG) since 1971 and has held every guild office, including that of president. He has received most of the guild's awards: the Robert Friedberg Award for literature in 1987, the Abe Kosoff Founder's Award in 1996, the Lifetime Achievement Award in 2000, and the Significant Contribution Award in 2003. He also created the Penny Board Project, which resulted in the distribution of $50,000 in scholarships and 250,000 coin boards to house Lincoln Memorial cents. As a result of that endeavor, he collaborated on a joint Quarter Board Project with the U.S. Mint and the PNG, which donated about 1,500,000 boards to young collectors.

A life member of the American Numismatic Association (ANA), Harlan has been on the editorial board of its official journal, *Numismatist*, for many years. He is chairman of the association's Roman Coin Project and has taught numerous summer seminars on ancient coins. His awards from the ANA include the Presidential Award (2001–2003) and the Glenn Smedley Award (2005).

A member and fellow of the American Numismatic Society, Harlan is also involved with the nonprofit project Ancient Coins for Education, which has named its highest teaching award after him—a rare honor for a living person. Among his other honors are the 2006 Numismatic Ambassador Award from Krause Publications and the Chicago Coin Club's 1996 Presidential Award, which he received for chairing the symposium "The Science of Numismatics" for the club and the American Numismatic Society of New York.

Harlan has written two books on Byzantine coins and about 100 articles, the first of which, "1802 Half Cent Struck on Large Cent," was published in the *Numismatic Scrapbook* in November 1965. He has won three numismatic literary awards—in 1989, 1990, and 1992—for his *World Coin News* column, "What's Old." He also authored the first ancient-coin section for *Gold Coins of the World*, by Arthur L. and Ira S. Friedberg.

Harlan is on the advisory boards of the World Heritage Museum (now the Spurlock Museum) at the University of Illinois and the Loyola University Museum of Art in Chicago, where he is also a founding member of the board. In his spare time he is creating a 160-acre sculpture park in Watervliet, Michigan, with the Zhou Brothers and his wife, Pamela. He also has a significant collection of paintings by Chicago artists from 1910 to 1950, published and exhibited by DePaul University in 2009.

ACKNOWLEDGMENTS

There are many people who aided me in the creation of this volume. The most important are David MacDonald and Curtis Clay. When I got stuck, David willingly spent a solid week with me in my office, which made it possible to get this project into gear. Curtis Clay, as most of the collecting community knows, is one of the best Roman scholars there is, and I am very lucky to have him in the next office. I also want to thank Phil Davis for the help he gave in the area of Roman Republican and Imperatorial coinage. I would like to thank Phil Davis, David MacDonald, and Curtis Clay for writing some of the first drafts of the essays in this book. Much gratitude goes to Ute Wartenberg Kagan of the American Numismatic Society, who is always there when you need her—and I needed her a lot. A special thanks to Arnold-Peter C. Weiss for his essay on the Syracusan tetradrachm of Alpheios. Very special thanks go to Alan Walker, Q. David Bowers, and Kenneth Bressett for their critical reading shortly before press time. Without our staff photographers Karen Block (now married and retired) and Holly Matthews (our present amazing talent),

as well as technical wizard Jake Smith, we would have no images—thus no book. In that vein, I gratefully acknowledge Christie's, Sotheby's, Numismatica Ars Classica, Classical Numismatic Group, LHS Numismatik, Bank Leu, Gemini, and Frank L. Kovacs for allowing me to use their images from past sales.

Special thanks go to Briggs Bralliar, Terry Wallenbrock, David Sundman, Mike Gasvoda, Jerry Bobbe, and Arnold-Peter C. Weiss, for photographing or allowing me to have their coins photographed for this volume. A thank-you also to Arthur Friedberg, for his titanic efforts to get us the image of the unique Aetna Master coin.

Thanks are also due to the members of my advisory committee, who helped me to pick the candidate coins for the voting. They are Rob Freeman, Frank Kovacs, Victor England, Arturo Russo, Alan Walker, and Simon Bendall. If you can think of another 100 coins that could have been in this book, I am with you all the way, but we aren't rewriting the British Museum Catalog.

I would like to thank everyone who actually voted on the coins to determine their ranking. They are Lawrence Adams, Peter Van Alfen, James Beach, Aaron Berk, Allen G. Berman, Eldert Bontekoe, Kenneth Bressett, Curtis Clay, Kirk Davis, Phillip Davis, Nicholas Economopoulos, Arthur Friedberg, Ira Goldberg, Bill Kalmbach, David MacDonald, Eric J. McFadden, Richard Ponterio, Jurgen Ritter, Douglass F. Rohrman, Jonathan Rosen, William Rosenblum, Wayne Sayles, Wayne Scheible, Shanna L. Schmidt, David Sear, Fred Shore, Jacob K. Stein, David Sundman, Alan Walker, and Arnold-Peter C. Weiss.

Of course, without the Greek and Roman civilizations, with their kings, emperors, armies, and usurpers—especially the usurpers—as well as the celators and slaves, we would never have these wonderful objects that illustrate 2,000 years of Western and Near Eastern history.

I must also thank the nice people at Whitman who asked me to do this project, and Jeff Garrett, who suggested me. My apologies to anyone whose contribution during this two-year project was overlooked in the thanks or credits.

CREDITS

Images for coins shown in the introduction (pages 1–8) are courtesy of Harlan J. Berk, Ltd., with the following exceptions: images of the Galba aureus, Vespasian aureus, and Diocletian argenteus (pages 2 and 3) are courtesy of Ira and Larry Goldberg Coins and Collectibles; images of the Widow's Mite (page 5) are from *Money of the Bible*, second edition, by Kenneth Bressett (2007).

The following coin images were graciously provided by LHS Numismatik: Nos. 4, 6 (primary image pair, page 35, and top supporting image pair, page 34), 7, 21, 29, 38, 59, 63, 66, 70 (primary image pair), 76, and 95.

The following coin images were graciously provided by Numismatic Ars Classica: Nos. 24, 53, 68, 71, 83, 86, 87, and 97.

Images of coin No. 5, the decadrachm (demareteion) of Syracuse with quadriga, appear courtesy of the Museum of Fine Arts, Boston (Theodora Wilbour Fund in memory of Zoë Wilbour, 35.21). Photography © 2007 Museum of Fine Arts, Boston.

Images of coin No. 22 are courtesy of Cabinet des Médailles, Brussels.

Images of coins Nos. 25, 42, 47, and 65 were graciously provided by the British Museum. Photos © The Trustees of the British Museum; all rights reserved.

Images of coin No. 32 are courtesy of Münzkabinett der Staatlichen Museen zu Berlin.

Images of coins Nos. 39, 41, and 100 are courtesy of Gemini, LLC.

Images of coin No. 48 are courtesy of Frank L. Kovacs.

Images of coin No. 61 (top image pair) are courtesy of Gorny and Mosch.

Images of coin No. 92 were graciously provided by Classical Numismatic Group, Ltd.

Photography of the following coins is by Karen Block of Harlan J. Berk, Ltd.: Nos. 1, 2, 3, 9, 10, 12, 14, 16 (all images), 18, 19, 26, 28, 31, 33, 34, 37, 40, 43, 45, 46, 49, 50, 54–58, 60, 64 (all images), 67, 70 (supporting image pair), 72, 74, 75 (all images), 77, 78, 80–82, 84, 89–91, 93, 94, and 98 (supporting image pair).

Photography of the following coins is by Holly Matthews of Harlan J. Berk, Ltd.: Nos. 11, 13, 15, 20, 23, 27 (all images), 44, 51, 52, 61 (lower image pair), 62, 69 (all images), 73, 79, 85, 88, 96 (all images), and 99.

Photography of coin No. 6 (page 34, lower image pair), from the collection of David Sundman, is by Stephanie Westover.

Photography of coin No. 17, from the collection of Arnold-Peter C. Weiss, is by Arnold-Peter C. Weiss.

Photography of coin No. 98 (primary image pair), from the collection of Jerry Bobbe, is by Larry Gaye.

Coin No. 13 is from the collection of Mike Gasvoda.
Coin No. 15 is from the collection of Sam Young.
Coin No. 28 is from the collection of Carl Subak.
Coin No. 73 is from the collection of Phillip Davis.
Coin No. 79 is from the collection of Terry Wallenbrock.
Coin No. 85 is from the collection of Mike Ruettgers.
Both coins shown in essay No. 96 are from the collection of Briggs Bralliar.

Images of coins Nos. 8, 35, and 36 are from the Sotheby's catalog *Nelson Bunker Hunt Collection* (1990); photos © Sotheby's. Images of coin No. 30 are from the Christie's catalog *Highly Important Ancient Coins* (1984); photos © Christie's.

Author portrait is © 2007 by Tom Maday.

If you enjoyed the history, romance, and artistry of the *100 Greatest Ancient Coins...*

…you'll also enjoy these interesting books from Whitman Publishing, available wherever books are sold.

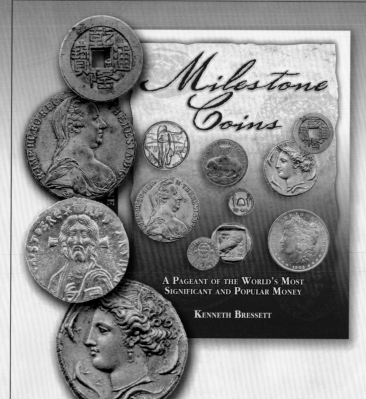

Milestone Coins is a collection of engaging stories and beautiful photographs of 110-plus popular coins and tokens. Your tour guide is Kenneth Bressett, longtime editor of the *Guide Book of United States Coins* (the famous "Red Book") and a legend in coin collecting. The book features ten chapters covering all time periods and geographical areas: The Ancient World; Biblical Coins; The Roman World; Medieval Europe; The World of Islam; Merry Olde England; The Reign in Spain; Cathay and the Orient; Emerging Concepts in Coinage; and Money in America.

Features include full-color, high-detail enlarged and actual-size photographs of each coin; smaller photos of varieties and related issues; market conditions; collecting tips; prices you can expect to pay; a comparative gallery of actual-size images; a bibliography; and an index with more than 800 entries.

Enjoy the art of coinage as never before, and learn some fascinating history along the way, in *Milestone Coins: A Pageant of the World's Most Significant and Popular Money.*

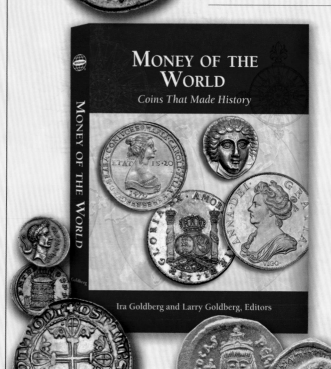

Editors Ira and Larry Goldberg have gathered six of the best numismatic historians to tell the story of Western Civilization, as seen through (and influenced by) some of the greatest coins in the world.

Money of the World: Coins That Made History features nearly 200 magnificent coins in both actual size and grand, full-color enlargement. Every detail is showcased: the totemic animals of ancient Greece; the dramatic portraits of the Renaissance; the defiant emblems of the United States' hard-won freedom. The coins reflect empire and colony, conquest and defiance, revolution and decline, godly splendor and human power. They tell their stories with unique voices. Look and listen, and you will learn the course of human history with a fresh new perspective.

Whitman Publishing, LLC
PUBLISHING SINCE 1934

www.whitman**books**.com

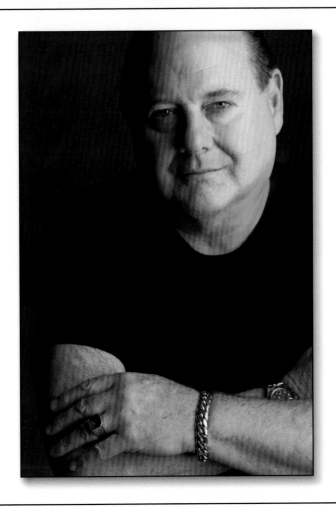